BLOOM'S ReViews

COMPREHENSIVE \ RESEARCH & STUDY GUIDES

Maya Angelou's
I Know Why the Caged Bird Sings

Edited & with
an Introduction
by Harold Bloom

First Printing
1 3 5 7 9 8 6 4 2

ISBN: 0-7910-4129-8

Chelsea House Publishers
1974 Sproul Road, Suite 400
P.O. Box 914
Broomall, PA 19008-0914

Contents

Editor's Note	4
Introduction	5
Biography of Maya Angelou	7
Thematic and Structural Analysis	10
List of Characters	22

Critical Views

Ernece B. Kelly: Angelou's Novel-Like Autobiography	24
Sidonie Ann Smith: The Opening Scene in Angelou's Autobiography	25
Annie Gottlieb: *Gather Together in My Name*	27
George E. Kent: The Unique Qualities of the Autobiography	28
Liliane K. Arensberg: Racial Self-Hatred	31
Adam David Miller: *The Heart of a Woman*	33
Sondra O'Neale: The Narrative Technique of Angelou's Autobiographies	35
Lucinda H. Mackethan: The Development of Angelou's Use of Language	37
Keneth Kinnamon: Angelou's Celebration of Black Culture	39
Christine Froula: Rape and its Aftermath	41
Mary Jane Lupton: Motherhood in Angelou's Autobiographies	43
Carol E. Neubauer: Angelou's Relationship with Her Mother	45
Dolly A. McPherson: The Importance of Angelou's Autobiographical Works	48
Mary Vermillion: Rape and Self-Expression	50
Onita Estes-Hicks: Angelou's Departure from the South	53
James Bertolino: Angelou's Honesty	54
Opal Moore: Opposition to the Autobiography	56
Works by Maya Angelou	60
Works about Maya Angelou and *I Know Why the Caged Bird Sings*	51
Index of Themes and Ideas	53

Editor's Note

My Introduction relates Maya Angelou's autobiography to a tradition of African-American religion. Critical Views begin with Sidonie Ann Smith's analysis of the opening scene and continue with Annie Gottlieb's review of *Gather Together in My Name*, the sequel to *I Know Why the Caged Bird Sings*. The fusion of blues and folk tradition in Angelou is studied by George E. Kent, after which Liliane K. Arensberg comments upon some of the opening fears in *Caged Bird*. A. D. Miller reviews *The Heart of a Woman*, Angelou's third autobiography, while Sondra O' Neale ponders the closeness of all the Angelou memoirs to narrative fiction. Angelou's language is the focus of Lucinda H. Mackethan, after which Keneth Kinnamon contrasts *Caged Bird* with Richard Wright's *Black Boy*, a rather less celebratory work.

The trauma of Angelou's rape at the age of eight is investigated by Christine Froula, while Mary Jane Lupton centers upon the image of motherhood in the autobiographies and Carol E. Neubauer deals directly with Angelou's relation with her own mother.

Dolly A. McPherson argues for the cultural importance of Angelou's autobiographies, after which Mary Vermillion considers the blocking effect of rape upon the victim's language and Onita Estes-Hicks reflects on Angelou's southern background.

James Bertolino praises Angelou for her striking candor, while Opal Moore concludes these extracts by defending *Caged Bird* as an exemplary work to be taught in the schools.

Introduction

HAROLD BLOOM

The popularity of *I Know Why the Caged Bird Sings* is proudly based upon its achieved pathos: It accomplishes a controlled poignance in representing a portrait of the artist as a young black woman. In the structural background of Maya Angelou's book hover the two prime traditional forms of African-American autobiography, the slave narrative and the African-American version of the church sermon. Each is at once individual and communal, with the two voices sometimes working with one another and sometimes impeding the other's full expression. Angelou, whatever her formal limitations as a poet, is a natural autobiographer who works with considerable skill and with narrative cunning. Her voice interweaves other strands in the African-American oral tradition, but the implicit forms of sermon and slave narrative are ghostly presences in her rhetoric. Angelou brings forward, with a rugged implicitness, a spiritual element vital to all indigenous American religion but original to the African-American paradigm of that religion. The early black Baptists in America spoke of "the little me within the big me," almost the last vestige of the spirituality they had carried with them on the Middle Passage from Africa. Converted to American Baptist Christianity, they brought to the slaveowner's faith a kind of gnosis, a radical knowing that "the little me" belonged not to the space and time of this harsh world but to an unfallen realm before the Creation-Fall of the whites. The sermonlike directness of *I Know Why the Caged Bird Sings* is empowered by Angelou's possession of this gnosis, which tells her always that what is best and oldest in her spirit goes back to a lost fullness of being.

Angelou's autobiographical tone is one of profound intimacy and radiates goodwill, even a serenity astonishingly at variance with the terrors and degradations she suffered as a child and as a very young woman. Her voice speaks to something in the American "little me within the big me," white and black and whatever, that can survive dreadful experiences because the deepest self is beyond experience and cannot be violated, even by such onslaughts as child abuse, rape, and prostitution. As we descend into the Age of Gingrich, where technocracy makes social compassion obsolete, the prospects for the continued relevance of *I Know Why the Caged Bird Sings* are only enhanced. Despite its secular mode, the book is a spiritual autobiography that addresses the popular imagination of a nation that does not understand its own religion, a Christian gnosis that has little in common with historical European Christianity. We have no history, only biography, and our biography has the single theme: survival of the innermost self. Maya Angelou, incarnating that theme, celebrates the immortality of a deepest self that was not born, and so cannot die, and is always being resurrected. ✤

Biography of Maya Angelou

Maya Angelou was born Marguerite Johnson in St. Louis, Missouri, on April 4, 1928. Her life has been both remarkably varied and occasionally grim (she was raped at the age of eight by her mother's boyfriend), and she has won greater critical acclaim for her several autobiographical volumes than for her poetry and drama. She attended public schools in Arkansas and California, studied music privately, and studied dance with Martha Graham. In 1954–55 she was a member of the cast of *Porgy and Bess,* which went on a twenty-two-nation world tour sponsored by the U.S. Department of State. Some of her songs were recorded on the album *Miss Calypso* (1957). Later she acted in several off-Broadway plays, including the musical *Cabaret for Freedom* (1960), which she wrote with Godfrey Cambridge.

In addition to these artistic pursuits, Angelou held a variety of odd jobs in her late teens and early twenties, including streetcar conductor, Creole cook, nightclub waitress, prostitute, and madam. She has been married twice: first, around 1950, to a white man, Tosh Angelos (whose surname she adapted when she became a dancer), and then, from 1973 to 1981, to Paul Du Feu. She bore a son, Guy, at the age of sixteen.

When she was thirty, Angelou moved to Brooklyn. There she met John Oliver Killens, James Baldwin, and other writers who encouraged her to write. While practicing her craft, however, she became involved in the civil rights movement. She met Martin Luther King, Jr., was appointed the northern coordinator of the Southern Christian Leadership Conference, and organized demonstrations at the United Nations. She fell in love with the South African freedom fighter Vusumzi Make, and they left for Egypt, where in 1961–62 Angelou worked as associate editor of the *Arab Observer,* an English-language newspaper in Cairo. She broke up with Make when he criticized her independence and lack of subservience to him.

In 1963 Angelou went to Ghana to be assistant administrator of the School of Music and Drama at the University of Ghana's Institute of African Studies. In the three years she was there she acted in several additional plays, served as feature editor of the *African Review,* and was a contributor to the Ghanaian Broadcasting Corporation. Returning to the United States, she was a lecturer at the University of California at Los Angeles and has subsequently been a visiting professor or writer in residence at several other universities.

Angelou's first published book was *I Know Why the Caged Bird Sings* (1969), an autobiography of the first sixteen years of her life; a tremendous critical and popular success, it was nominated for a National Book Award and was later adapted for television. Two more autobiographical volumes appeared in the 1970s, *Gather Together in My Name* (1974) and *Singin' and Swingin' and Gettin' Merry Like Christmas* (1976), along with three volumes of poetry: *Just Give Me a Cool Drink of Water 'fore I Diiie* (1971), *Oh Pray My Wings Are Gonna Fit Me Well* (1975), and *And Still I Rise* (1978). She wrote several more dramas, including the unpublished *And Still I Rise!,* a medley of black poetry and music that was successfully staged in 1976; two screenplays (directing one of them and writing the musical scores for both); and several television plays, including a series of ten one-hour programs entitled *Blacks, Blues, Black.* She also continued to pursue her acting career and was nominated for a Tony Award in 1973 for her Broadway debut, *Look Away.* She was appointed a member of the American Revolution Bicentennial Council by President Gerald R. Ford in 1975.

In the last fifteen years Angelou has solidified her reputation with two more autobiographies, *The Heart of a Woman* (1981) and *All God's Children Need Traveling Shoes* (1986), along with two more volumes of poetry, *Shaker, Why Don't You Sing?* (1983) and *I Shall Not Be Moved* (1990). The peak of her fame was perhaps achieved when in 1993 she composed a poem, "On the Pulse of Morning," for the inauguration of President Bill Clinton. Angelou's latest prose work, *Wouldn't Take Nothing for My Journey Now,* a collection of essays and sketches, also appeared in 1993 and, like most of its predecessors, was a best-seller.

Maya Angelou, who has received honorary degrees from Smith College, Mills College, and Lawrence University, currently resides in Sonoma, California. ❖

Thematic and Structural Analysis

I Know Why the Caged Bird Sings opens with Maya Angelou remembering herself as a young child trying to recite a poem to the Colored Methodist Episcopal Church in Stamps, Arkansas. Overcome with shame for forgetting the lines, Angelou—or Marguerite Johnson, as she was then called—runs from the church amid the other children's laughter. This incident establishes the narrative approach of Angelou's memoir: *I Know Why the Caged Bird Sings* is a collection of distinct episodes strung together chronologically. The opening account of Angelou's public humiliation in the church also foreshadows some of the fundamental challenges that faced a young black girl growing up in the racist America of the 1930s and 1940s. Uncertainty and the constant threat of degradation thwart even the most precocious, determined child: "If growing up is painful for the Southern Black girl, being aware of her displacement is the rust on the razor that threatens the throat. It is an unnecessary insult." Angelou's keen attention to details, such an effective element in the memoir, may indeed have once been her childhood strategy to combat the pain of her situations. Vividly recalling them years later seems to be Angelou's way of accepting or reclaiming her experiences, of authoring her own life. Angelou is also aware that her private recollections form more than an autobiography of an individual: They form the story of a people and a time.

Angelou begins her narrative (**chapter one**) with perhaps her earliest memory, when she is three and her brother, Bailey, Jr., is four. Their parents end their "calamitous" marriage and send the children by train—with "To Whom It May Concern" instructions tagged on their wrists—from Long Beach, California, to Stamps, Arkansas. There they live with their paternal grandmother, Mrs. Annie Henderson, and with their uncle Willie, who was crippled as a baby when he was dropped by a babysitter (**chapter two**). Sister Henderson, as their grandmother is called by the town, is a sternly religious and hardworking woman who owns a general store and is well respected by the segregated community. Bailey and Marguerite call her Momma.

Each morning Momma wakes at four to tend the Store (always "spoken of with a capital *s*") and wait on the people who gather there in the hopeful morning darkness before being taken to pick cotton in the fields. One day (**chapter three**) the white former sheriff nonchalantly rides on horseback to the Store to tell Annie that she had better warn Uncle Willie to "lay low" because a black man has "messed with a white lady," so "some of the boys" will surely come around. Marguerite thinks of those "cement faces and eyes of hate that burned the clothes off you" and wonders how the sheriff could refer to such evil, violently bigoted men as "boys."

Chapters four through seven recount more of Marguerite's early life in Stamps and her constant awareness of racial difference. She describes her brother, Bailey, as the greatest person in her world, the only one who can make her feel better when even the adults insult her looks. On errands for their grandmother, she and Bailey venture together beyond their known world into dangerous "whitefolksville." Because segregation is so restrictive and prejudice so intense, black children have little contact with whites. Angelou remembers "never believing that whites were really real." Distinct from "whitefolks," however, are "powhitetrash." Because her grandmother owns and rents a few houses on her farmland, Marguerite does have contact with the disrespectful and unkempt "powhitetrash" children who live there and boss Marguerite's grandmother around the Store without even addressing her as Mrs. Henderson.

One time the white children taunt and jeer Momma, mocking her mannerisms and mooning her from the front yard, while Momma simply stands on the porch singing a slow hymn to herself. At first Marguerite is humiliated, especially when her grandmother politely says good-bye to the impudent children, but shortly thereafter she realizes her grandmother's self-respect means she has "won" the encounter. Momma is to Marguerite a formidable figure of "power and strength. She [is] taller than any woman in [Marguerite's] personal world, . . . and her voice [is] soft only because she [chooses] to keep it so."

Although Marguerite's grandmother has "more money than all the powhitetrash," she too is hit by the Depression, which seeps "into the Black area slowly, like a thief with misgivings." One Christmas during the Depression (**chapter eight**), Marguerite and her brother receive gifts from their mother and father, who live separately in "a heaven called California." This unexpected contact with their parents—whom Marguerite has assumed are dead, going so far as to picture her unknown mother in a coffin with her black hair "spread out on a tiny little white pillow"—frightens and confuses both children. What had they done so wrong to be sent away?

A year later (**chapter nine**) their father, Daddy Bailey, shows up unannounced in Stamps, and Marguerite's "seven-year-old world humpty-dumptied, never to be put back together again." She is afraid of her father, a big, broad-shouldered, handsome, and vain man who speaks "proper English" and is the "first cynic" she has ever met. But she is proud too: "Everyone could tell from the way he talked and from the car and clothes that he was rich and maybe had a castle out in California." When he reveals that he is taking the children to St. Louis to live with their mother, Marguerite and Bailey panic.

St. Louis is "a new kind of hot and a new kind of dirty." But when the children at last meet their "Mother Dear" they are entranced by her physical beauty. "To describe my mother would be to write about a hurricane in its perfect power. Or the climbing, falling colors of a rainbow," writes Angelou. But upon seeing her, the young Marguerite understands at once why she earlier sent her children away: "She was too beautiful to have children." Vivian Baxter is a cool and vivacious woman who sings in a tavern, plays poker in illegal gambling parlors, and comes from a family of brothers known about town for their "unrelenting meanness." Despite their bad reputation, though, these uncles give the young Marguerite a sense of family and even of worth: "[D]on't worry 'cause you ain't pretty," says one. "Plenty pretty women I seen digging ditches or worse. You smart." They also tell her how she got her name: Her brother originally insisted on calling her "Mya Sister," eventually transformed to "Maya" (**chapter ten**).

After staying a while with Grandmother Baxter, the children eventually move in with their mother and her boyfriend, Mr. Freeman. They each have a "room with a two-sheeted bed, plenty to eat and store-bought clothes to wear." Yet these luxuries lie like a burden upon the anxious Marguerite, whose fear of being suddenly ejected again clogs her "childish wits into impassivity."

At eight years of age, Marguerite sleeps with her mother and Mr. Freeman when she has nightmares (**chapters eleven through thirteen**). One morning after her mother has left, Mr. Freeman molests Marguerite. She is confused and afraid of how rapidly Mr. Freeman's heart is beating as he holds her to his chest, but she likes being held close and mistakenly interprets the tight embrace as love. Mr. Freeman threatens to kill her brother if she tells anyone what "they" did, and this confuses the child even more: "It was the same old quandary. I had always lived it. There was an army of adults, whose motives and movements I just couldn't understand and who made no effort to understand mine." In her ignorance, though, Marguerite begins to "feel lonely for Mr. Freeman and the encasement of his big arms. Before, [her] world [was] Bailey, food, Momma, the Store, reading books and Uncle Willie. Now, for the first time, it [includes] physical contact." The incident is repeated, although Mr. Freeman later ignores Marguerite. She eventually puts the episode aside and devotes herself to reading: Horatio Alger, Shakespeare, Kipling, Poe, Langston Hughes, James Weldon Johnson, and W. E. B. Du Bois have captivated her. She "breathes in the world of penniless shoeshine boys, . . . little princesses who were mistaken for maids, and the long-lost children mistaken for waifs."

But some time later, perhaps in retribution for her mother's absence the previous night, Mr. Freeman rapes Marguerite, which Angelou describes as a "breaking and entering when even the senses are torn apart." When the eight-year-old girl returns to consciousness, he is washing her in the bathtub and, although apologizing for hurting her, repeats his threat to kill Bailey if she tells anyone. Marguerite hides her bloodstained underwear under her mattress and goes to bed. But a day later the underwear is discovered and Marguerite is taken to the hospital, where she tells her brother the name of the rapist.

Mr. Freeman is arrested and so "spared the awful wrath of [Marguerite's] pistol-whipping uncles." Later he is tried in public, but Marguerite cannot admit that he had earlier molested her: That fact, she believes, implicates her in the rape. He is sentenced to a year and a day in prison but is released the same afternoon. Later that day, however, his body is found on a vacant lot. To the traumatized child, her lie becomes the cause of Mr. Freeman's death. Marguerite believes she has sold herself to the devil: "I could feel the evilness flowing through my body and waiting, pent up, to rush off my tongue if I tried to open my mouth." She decides she must stop talking to everyone but her brother because "just [her] breath, carrying [her] words out, might poison people and they'd curl up and die like the black fat slugs that only pretended." Less than a year after they arrived, Bailey and his mute, incomprehensible sister are sent back to Stamps to live with their paternal grandmother again.

Chapters fourteen through sixteen recount Marguerite's return to the "barrenness of Stamps" and the small, quiet world of the Store and Momma. There "[s]ounds come to [her] dully, as if people were speaking through their handkerchiefs or with their hands over their mouths. Colors weren't true either. . . ." Bailey makes up for his sister's continued silence by telling fanciful stories of fast-paced city life up north. Marguerite keeps to herself in the slow "cocoon" of Stamps, where nothing ever happens, until one day Mrs. Bertha Flowers, the "aristocrat of Black Stamps," takes an interest in her.

To Marguerite, Mrs. Flowers is like "women in English novels who. . . . [walk] over the 'heath' and read morocco-bound books and [have] two last names divided by a hyphen." She is well spoken, refined, and formally educated. On occasion it upsets Marguerite to see her grandmother speaking informally to the woman Marguerite sees as the more sophisticated, but the two adults understand and respect each other. Mrs. Flowers helps Marguerite overcome her reticence by sharing her own love for literature and poetry, particularly when recited. She gives Marguerite "lessons in living," which include reading her favorite works aloud to Marguerite and asking the girl to do the same. She also has Marguerite memorize and recite poetry and teaches her to "be intolerant of ignorance but understanding of illiteracy."

Shortly thereafter Marguerite is given a job as a cook's helper in a white woman's kitchen. Learning that her employer, Mrs. Cullinan, cannot have children, Marguerite initially has sympathy for her and pities her further for being apparently unable to pronounce Marguerite's name (Mrs. Cullinan calls her "Margaret"). But when Mrs. Cullinan takes a friend's advice and now begins to call Marguerite "Mary" for even greater simplicity, Marguerite deliberately breaks the woman's most cherished dishes and is fired.

One Saturday night, when eleven-year-old Bailey doesn't come home till long after dark, his family fears he may have become another victim of white racism. Describing Momma's fears especially, Angelou writes, "The Black woman in the South who raises sons, grandsons and nephews had her heartstrings tied to a hanging noose" (**chapter seventeen**). When he finally returns, there is "no air of spent revelry about him," but he is severely whipped by Uncle Willie. It isn't for several days—during which his eyes are "vacant" and it seems "his soul [has] flown away"—that he tells Marguerite the reason for his lateness. In a film, he has seen "a white movie star who looks just like Mother Dear." Although Marguerite, when she too has seen this actress, thinks that it is "extraordinary good fortune to be able to save up one's money and go see one's mother whenever one [wants] to," Bailey is made emotional and reckless by the imagined proximity.

Chapter eighteen details a revival meeting held one weekday night and attended by members of all the local churches.

> People whose history and future were threatened each day by extinction considered that it was only by divine intervention that they were able to live at all. . . . but as human beings become more affluent, as their living standard and style begin to ascend the material scale, God descends the scale of responsibility at a commensurate speed.

Describing this event, Angelou becomes outraged at her people for allowing themselves "to be worked like oxen" and who not only are fated "to live the poorest, roughest life," but actually seem to prefer it. But the preacher's sermon on charity, in which he praises the righteousness of the poor (whom the congregants take to be themselves) and damns the arrogance of the rich (who are clearly white), also tries to make sense of the listeners' poverty and oppression and strengthens their sense of community. People "who only a few hours earlier had crumbled in [the Store's] front yard, defeated by the cotton rows, now sat on the edges of their rickety-rackety chairs. Their faces shone with the delight of their souls. The mean whitefolks was going to get their comeuppance."

In **chapter nineteen** Angelou remembers the night heavyweight boxer Joe Louis, a black man, fights a white opponent for the world championship. All the inhabitants of Stamps come to the Store until every "inch of space is filled," and Uncle Willie turns the radio "up to its last notch so that youngsters on the porch wouldn't miss a word." Everyone listens nervously as the symbol of their community boxes in the ring. It is as if the pride and self-esteem of all blacks rests upon Louis's victory. For if he loses, it "would all be true, the accusations that [blacks] were lower types of human beings." In winning, Angelou observes, Louis "proved that we were the strongest people in the world."

The incidents next described (**chapters twenty through twenty-two**) are important for Marguerite's emotional and spiritual development. At the town's summer picnic, during which Marguerite feels so out of place she even wanders into a secluded grove to relieve herself because she cannot follow the signs saying either WOMEN or CHILDREN, Marguerite is discovered by the equally lonely and imaginative Louise Kendricks. Louise, whose face is "long and dark chocolate brown" with "a thin sheet of sadness over it," becomes Marguerite's first childhood friend. Together the two girls play, create their own secret language, and giggle over the important matters of boys and life. Through their friendship Marguerite learns how to be a child and to forget the adult trauma of St. Louis and Mr. Freeman.

At the same time, Marguerite's brother has taken to playing "Momma and Poppa" with girls in the neighborhood until he comes upon a country girl named Joyce who is four years his senior and does more than play-act. She becomes Bailey's first girlfriend, "his first love outside the family." When she eventually leaves, Marguerite looks on as Bailey closes "in upon himself like a pond swallowing a stone."

In addition to beginning to learn about sex and attachments, Marguerite at eleven has her first realization of the finality of death when Miz Florida, the wife of forty years to a Mr. George Taylor, dies and bequeaths a brooch to Marguerite. Momma forces Marguerite to go to the funeral, where the sight of the dead woman's face, "empty and evil," "deflated and patted flat like a cow's ordurous dropping," haunts her: "Instantly I surrendered myself to the grimness of death." At dinner one night six months later, Mr. Taylor insists to Marguerite and her family that he has heard his wife's ghost the previous night. This frightens the whole family, particularly Marguerite, despite—or perhaps because of—Momma's intense religious belief.

Marguerite's graduation from the eighth grade recalls the opening scene of reciting a poem in church (**chapter twenty-three**). For months all of Stamps looks forward to the graduation ceremony with pride, and, because of her achievements and awards, Marguerite is especially proud. At the ceremony, however, a white politician running for election humiliates everyone by cataloging his many improvements to the educational facilities at the white schools—yet promising only a paved sports field to the black school in Stamps. Marguerite is deflated by the injustice: "It was awful to be a Negro and have no control over my life. It was brutal to be young and already trained to sit quietly and listen to charges brought against my color with no chance of defense." But Henry Reed, the class valedictorian, rekindles hope when he leads his classmates, and soon the audience, in singing what Angelou calls the Negro national anthem, James Weldon Johnson's "Lift Ev'ry Voice and Sing":

> Stony the road we trod
> Bitter the chastening rod
> Felt in the days when hope, unborn, had died.
> Yet with a steady beat
> Have not our weary feet
> Come to the place for which our fathers sighed?

In **chapter twenty-four** Marguerite is subjected to more immediate and personal racism when the white dentist in Stamps refuses to treat her severe toothache. He says he would rather stick his hand in "a dog's mouth than in a nigger's," even though Marguerite's grandmother loaned him money during the Depression. They are instead obliged to travel twenty-five miles to the nearest black dentist.

Finally (**chapter twenty-five**), Momma decides to take her grandchildren back to their parents in California, a decision she may have reached after Bailey watched the rotting body of a black man pulled from the pond and saw a white man stand grinning over the corpse.

Momma takes Marguerite to Los Angeles to her mother and lives with them until Bailey comes a month later. **Chapters twenty-six through twenty-nine** chronicle their reunion and subsequent move to San Francisco, where both children are again enchanted by their "beautiful and wild mother." In the early months of World War II, the Japanese population in San Francisco is removed "soundlessly and without protest," while blacks, particularly those just arrived from the South, move in. For many reasons the new arrivals are indifferent to the plight of the displaced Japanese, largely because they may be so overwhelmed by their own new opportunities. Marguerite revels in the freedom and anonymity of the city: To "a thirteen-year-old Black girl, stalled by the South and Southern Black life style, the city was a state of beauty and a state of freedom."

Marguerite is sent to an almost entirely white high school, where by one teacher at least she is treated exactly as the white students are. At fourteen years of age, Marguerite wins a scholarship to a local college and attends evening dance and drama classes for adults. She also learns to play poker and blackjack from her mother's new husband, Daddy Clidell, "a simple man who [has] no inferiority complex about his lack of education and, even more amazing, no superiority complex because he [has] succeeded despite that lack." Through him Marguerite meets "the most colorful characters in the Black underground" and comes to understand the ethics, and even glories, of hustling white people. Just as there are different languages spoken in the white and black communities, Angelou says, there is a different understanding of justice.

Marguerite's experiences in Southern California are told in **chapters thirty through thirty-two**. She begins her summer vacation by joining her father in his trailer home, where he lives with his jealous and insecure girlfriend, Dolores Stockland, whom Marguerite finds "mean and petty and full of pretense." Dolores becomes even more jealous when Daddy Bailey takes only his daughter on one of his frequent trips to Mexico. Marguerite is excited by his rare show of affection for her, and in a Mexican cantina she sees a new side of her father: He is relaxed and speaks without his usual affectation. Apparently the Mexicans have a genuine regard for him; here he is an important man. Marguerite, too, is accepted and delights in the festive atmosphere.

But after dancing and eating, Marguerite notices that her father has left the crowded cantina. She wonders whether her father has sold her to the Mexicans and left her for good, but when she sees his car still parked outside she realizes he must have gone off with one of the many women who were so happy to see him upon their arrival. Eventually her drunken father is walked back to the car and passes out in the back seat, so Marguerite tries to drive home even though she has never driven before. She navigates fifty miles successfully but runs into another car at the border.

Upon their return to the trailer home, fighting breaks out, first between Dolores and Daddy Bailey, who promptly leaves, and then between Dolores and Marguerite. Dolores calls Marguerite's mother "a whore," Marguerite slaps her, and Dolores in turn cuts the girl. Marguerite believes she is going to die but is bandaged by one of her father's friends. She spends the night with another of his friends, but in the morning, realizing that she and everyone else would be relieved if she "disappeared," she sets out alone.

That night Marguerite comes upon a junkyard, where she sleeps in a vacant car. In the morning she is surprised to find that the junkyard is inhabited by other orphaned and runaway children, each sleeping in his or her own car. Marguerite spends a month living and working odd jobs with the other children—among whom she learns "to drive . . . to curse and to dance"—before deciding that she is ready to return home to her mother. The month living communally, sharing chores and money with peers of all races, fosters a strong sense of belonging and sets a pattern of tolerance Angelou tries to follow.

Back with her mother—who, she declares defiantly, is "a fine lady" (**chapter thirty-three**)—Marguerite understands that her time in Southern California has put an end to whatever childhood innocence and insecurity she had left: "Without willing it, I had gone from being ignorant of being ignorant to being aware of being aware." Bailey, too, in the interim, has left his boyhood. He now dresses in zoot suits, talks like his streetwise new friends, and has even "acquired a withered white prostitute." After many arguments with his mother, with whom he is "entangled in the Oedipal skein," Bailey leaves home at the age of sixteen.

In **chapter thirty-four** Marguerite believes that it is time for her also to become more adult and independent. She decides she wants a job as a streetcar conductor. However, up to this time, blacks were not allowed to work on the streetcars. Angelou explains, "The Black female is assaulted in her tender years . . . [by] the tripartite crossfire of masculine prejudice, white illogical hate and Black lack of power." But with stubborn attempts and her mother's quiet encouragement, Marguerite is finally hired as the first black on San Francisco's streetcars.

The memoir's concluding episodes (**chapters thirty-five and thirty-six**) recount Marguerite's adolescent initiation into adult sexuality and motherhood. She reads *The Well of Loneliness* and, because of her own deep voice, large feet, and small breasts, begins to fear she may be a lesbian. Out of desperation she consults her mother, who reassures her that the changes she is going through are a result of puberty. However, when Marguerite happens to see a female friend undress and is awestruck by the beauty of her friend's breasts, she again wonders. To placate her fears, Marguerite asks a boy to have sex with her. He does, without question or care, and Marguerite soon finds she is pregnant from the "strange and strangely empty night."

Marguerite successfully hides her pregnancy from everyone around her for eight months, until she has safely received her high school diploma. Without any condemnation, her mother agrees that Marguerite and the father should not marry if neither wants to. Shortly thereafter Marguerite has a baby boy. "He was beautiful and mine," Angelou writes. "Totally mine." She ends her narrative with the image of Marguerite sleeping in bed with her newborn, covering him protectively with her arm and blanket—and thus the memoir moves full circle from an image of a powerless and frightened girl to one of a newly mature woman, in turn sheltering a child. ❖

—*Michael R. Steinberg*
New York University

List of Characters

Marguerite Johnson is Maya Angelou as she remembers herself for the first sixteen years of her life. She is called "Sister" by her grandmother, "Maya" by her brother Bailey, and "Ritie" by her mother. The "tender-hearted" child is awkward, withdrawn, and precocious. But her awareness and sensitivity are frequently frustrated by her inability to understand the adult world, particularly the male, white world beyond the small community of Stamps, Arkansas. Through each experience Marguerite tries to overcome her self-consciousness, feel that she belongs in the world, and do what is right.

Bailey Johnson, Jr., is Marguerite's elder brother. Having been sent together by their parents to be raised by their grandmother, Bailey and Maya offer each other constant support and companionship. They share their love for reading and their attempts to understand the world around them.

Momma (Mrs. Annie Henderson) is Marguerite's paternal grandmother, who raises the young girl and her brother. She owns a general store and is a respected figure in Stamps. She is rarely affectionate or emotional, and Marguerite is often punished for transgressing her grandmother's strict religious beliefs, many of which the child does not understand. Still, Momma's overbearing presence and self-respect guide Marguerite and give her a sense of strength and safety.

Uncle Willie is Marguerite's uncle, Annie Henderson's other son. Uncle Willie was crippled at the age of three when a babysitter dropped him. As a result he is unmarried and childless and lives with Momma at the Store. The unfairness of his handicap impresses itself upon Marguerite at an early age.

Daddy Bailey is Marguerite's father. He is a big, handsome man who speaks with affectation. He figures in the memoir principally through his distance, both physical and emotional, and through his role in bringing Bailey and Marguerite to live with their mother after being raised by their grandmother.

Mother Dear (Vivian Baxter) is Marguerite's mother. Her animated personality confuses and enthralls Marguerite, who describes her as a beautiful woman with a fierce temper when slighted. (She shot a "business partner" twice for cursing her.) She is a fast-talking, quick-witted, and well-liked gambler about town, and her love for Marguerite is never in question.

Mr. Freeman is an early boyfriend of Marguerite's mother. While Bailey and Marguerite live with them, Mr. Freeman molests and eventually rapes Marguerite. Though he is sentenced to a year in jail, he is released the day of the trial and is found dead later that afternoon.

Mrs. Bertha Flowers (Sister Flowers) is a refined woman in Stamps whose interest in Marguerite helps her overcome her silence. By reciting poetry and encouraging Marguerite to do the same, the formally educated woman teaches her the beauty of spoken language.

Louise Kendricks is Marguerite's first real childhood friend. She is intelligent and well behaved, and Marguerite considers her almost as pretty as Mrs. Flowers. Through her friendship with Louise, Marguerite regains childhood happiness and, in part, innocence.

Dolores Stockland lives with Daddy Bailey in his trailer home in Southern California. Her violent jealousy of Marguerite causes the girl to run away and live for a month with other children in an abandoned junkyard.

Daddy Clidell is the successful businessman who marries Marguerite's mother when she and Bailey live with her in California. Marguerite admires him for being a simple man who is neither insecure nor proud of his lack of formal education. ❖

Critical Views

[*I Know Why the Caged Bird Sings* did not receive
many reviews when it appeared in 1969. In the following review, Ernece B. Kelly, a professor of English at
Kingsborough Community College in Brooklyn, New
York, finds the work almost novel-like in its depiction of
the varied scenes of Angelou's childhood.]

Miss Angelou confidently reaches back in memory to pull out
the painful childhood times: when children fail to break the
adult code, disastrously breaching faith and laws they know
nothing of; when the very young swing easy from hysterical
laughter to awful loneliness; from a hunger for heroes to the
voluntary Pleasure-Pain game of wondering who their *real* parents are and how long before they take them to their authentic
home.

Introducing herself as Marguerite, a "tender-hearted" child,
the author allows her story to range in an extraordinary fashion
along the field of human emotion. With a child's fatalism, a
deep cut ushers in visions of an ignoble death. With a child's
addiction to romance and melodrama, she imagines ending her
life in the dirt-yard of a Mexican family—among strangers! It is
as if Miss Angelou has a Time Machine, so unerringly does she
record the private world of the young where sin is the Original
Sin and embarrassment, penultimate. 〈. . .〉

Miss Angelou accommodates her literary style to the various
settings her story moves through. She describes a rural
vignette which is "sweet-milk fresh in her memory . . ." and a
San Francisco rooming house where "Chicken suppers and
gambling games were rioting on a twenty-four hour basis
downstairs." Her metaphors are strong and right; her similes
less often so. But these lapses in poetic style are undeniably
balanced by the insight she offers into the effects of social con-
ditioning on the life-style and self-concept of a Black child
growing up in the rural South of the 1930's.

This is a novel about Blackness, youth, and white American society, usually in conflict. The miracle is that out of the War emerges a whole person capable of believing in her worth and capabilities. On balance, it is a gentle indictment of white American womanhood. It is a timely book.

—Ernece B. Kelly, [Review of *I Know Why the Caged Bird Sings*], *Harvard Educational Review* 40, No. 4 (November 1970): 681–82

❖

SIDONIE ANN SMITH ON THE OPENING SCENE IN ANGELOU'S AUTOBIOGRAPHY

[Sidonie Ann Smith is a professor of English at the State University of New York at Binghamton. She has written *A Poetics of Women's Autobiography* (1987) and *Subjectivity, Identity, and the Body: Women's Autobiographical Practices in the Twentieth Century* (1993). In this extract, Smith studies the opening scene of *I Know Why the Caged Bird Sings*, showing that it establishes the themes of entrapment and freedom that structure the entire work.]

Maya Angelou's autobiography, like ⟨Richard⟩ Wright's ⟨*Black Boy*⟩, opens with a primal childhood scene that brings into focus the nature of the imprisoning environment from which the self will seek escape. The black girl child is trapped within the cage of her own diminished self-image around which interlock the bars of natural and social forces. The oppression of natural forces, of physical appearance and processes, foists a self-consciousness on all young girls who must grow from children into women. Hair is too thin or stringy or mousy or nappy. Legs are too fat, too thin, too bony, the knees too bowed. Hips are too wide or not wide enough. Breasts grow too fast or not at all. The self-critical process is incessant, a driving demon. But in the black girl child's experience these natural bars are reinforced with the rusted iron social bars of racial subordination and impotence. Being born black is itself a liability in a world ruled by white standards of beauty which imprison the child *a priori* in a cage of ugliness: "What you looking at me for?" This really isn't me. I'm white with long blond hair and blue eyes, with pretty pink skin and straight hair, with a delicate mouth. I'm my own mistake. I haven't dreamed myself hard enough. I'll try again. The black and blue bruises of the soul multiply and compound as the caged bird flings herself against these bars:

> The Black female is assaulted in her tender years by all those common forces of nature at the same time that she is caught in the tripartite crossfire of masculine prejudice, white illogical hate and Black lack of power.

Within this imprisoning environment there is no place for this black girl child. She becomes a displaced person whose pain is intensified by her consciousness of that displacement:

> If growing up is painful for the Southern Black girl, being aware of her displacement is the rust on the razor that threatens the throat.
> It is an unnecessary insult.

If the black man is denied his potency and his masculinity, if his autobiography narrates the quest of the black male after a "place" of full manhood, the black woman is denied her beauty and her quest is one after self-accepted black womanhood. Thus the discovered pattern of significant moments Maya Angelou superimposes on the experience of her life is a pattern of moments that trace the quest of the black female after a "place," a place where a child no longer need ask self-consciously, "What you looking at me for?" but where a woman can declare confidently, "I am a beautiful, Black woman."

> —Sidonie Ann Smith, "The Song of a Caged Bird: Maya Angelou's Quest After Self-Acceptance," *Southern Humanities Review* 7, No. 4 (Fall 1973): 368

[Annie Gottlieb, a cultural critic and author, has written *Do You Believe in Magic? The Coming of the Sixties Generation* (1987) and, with Thomas McKnight, *Voyage to Paradise: A Visual Odyssey* (1993). In this extract, Gottlieb reviews *Gather Together in My Name*, comparing it with its predecessor.]

Gather Together in My Name is a little shorter and thinner than its predecessor; telling of an episodic, searching and wandering period in Maya Angelou's life, it lacks the density of childhood. In full compensation, her style has both ripened and simplified. It is more telegraphic and more condensed, transmitting a world of sensation or emotion or understanding in one image—in short, it is more like poetry. (Maya Angelou published a book of poems, *Just Give Me a Cool Drink of Water 'Fore I Diiie*, in between the two autobiographical volumes.) ⟨. . .⟩

In *Gather Together in My Name*, the ridiculous and touching posturing of a young girl in the throes of growing up are superimposed on the serious business of survival and responsibility for a child. Maya Angelou's insistence on taking full responsibility for her own life, her frank and humorous examination of her self, will challenge many a reader to be as honest under easier circumstances. Reading her book, you may learn, too, the embrace and ritual, the dignity and solace and humor of the black community. You will meet strong, distinctive people, drawn with deftness and compassion; their blackness is not used to hide their familiar but vulnerable humanity any more than their accessible humanity can for a moment be used to obscure their blackness—or their oppression. Maya Angelou's second book about her life as a young black woman in America is engrossing and vital, rich and funny and wise.

—Annie Gottlieb, "Growing Up and the Serious Business of Survival," *New York Times Book Review*, 16 June 1974, pp. 16, 20

GEORGE E. KENT ON THE UNIQUE QUALITIES OF *I KNOW WHY THE CAGED BIRD SINGS*

[George E. Kent is the author of *A Life of Gwendolyn Brooks* (1990). In this extract, Kent argues that *I Know Why the Caged Bird Sings* holds a unique place in black autobiography because of its rich imaginative qualities and its handling of the relationship between the individual and society.]

I Know Why creates a unique place within black autobiographical tradition, not by being "better" than the formidable autobiographical landmarks described, but by its special stance toward the self, the community, and the universe, and by a form exploiting the full measure of imagination necessary to acknowledge both beauty and absurdity.

The emerging self, equipped with imagination, resourcefulness, and a sense of the tenuousness of childhood innocence, attempts to foster itself by crediting the adult world with its own estimate of its god-like status and managing retreats into the autonomy of the childhood world when conflicts develop. Given the black adult's necessity to compromise with prevailing institutions and to develop limited codes through which nobility, strength, and beauty can be registered, the areas where a child's requirements are absolute—love, security, and consistency—quickly reveal the protean character of adult support and a barely concealed, aggressive chaos.

We can divide the adults' resources, as they appear in the autobiography, into two areas of black life: the religious and blues traditions. Grandmother Henderson, of Stamps, Arkansas, represents the religious traditions; Mother Vivian Baxter, more of the blues-street tradition.

Grandmother's religion gives her power to order her being, that of the children, and usually the immediate space surrounding her. The spirit of the religion combined with simple, traditional maxims shapes the course of existence and the rituals of facing up to something called decency. For Maya and her brother Bailey, the first impact of the blues-street tradition is that of instability: at the ages of three and four, respectively, the children are suddenly shipped to Grandmother when the parents break up their "calamitous" marriage. A note "To Whom It May Concern" identifies the children traveling alone from "Long Beach, California, en route to Stamps, Arkansas, c/o Mrs. Annie Henderson." Angelou generalizes the children's situation as follows: "Years later I discovered that the United States had been crossed thousands of times by frightened Black children traveling alone to their newly affluent parents in Northern cities, or back to grandmothers in Southern towns when the urban North reneged on its economic promises."

Gradually, the children adjust to the new life, becoming an integral part of Grandmother Henderson's General Merchandise Store, Grandmother's church and religion, community school, and general community customs. In Chapters 1–8, we see the techniques by which the author is able to give a full registration of both the beauty and the root absurdity built into the traditions of the folk community. She carefully articulates the folk forms of responding to existence by the use of key symbols and patterns of those involved in religious and blues responses and the joining point between their ways of responding. For example, more than Grandmother Henderson is characterized through the following folk prayer, whose set phrases have accreted through a long tradition of bended knees in homes and small rural churches:

> "Our Father, thank you for letting me see this New Day. Thank you that you didn't allow the bed I lay on last night to be my cooling board, nor my blanket my winding sheet. Guide my feet this day along the straight and narrow, and help me to put a bridle on my tongue. Bless this house, and everybody in it. Thank you, in the name of your Son, Jesus Christ, Amen."

The children are required to avoid impudence to adults, to respect religious piety, and to be obedient. Given the freshness of the childhood imagination, however, many meanings are turned into the absurdity often hovering near the fabric of human rituals. On the grim side, we see the poor giving thanks to the Lord for a life filled with the most meager essentials and a maximum amount of brute oppression. The church rituals create for the poor a temporary transcendence and an articulation of spirit, but their hardships are so graphically awaiting their reconfrontation with the trials of daily existence that the evoked spiritual beauty seems hard-pressed by the pathos of the grotesque. Still, it is from such religious rhythms that Grandmother Henderson possesses the strength to give much order to the children's lives, to set the family in initial order in California, and to provide them with the minimum resources to struggle for a world more attractive. The comic side is reflected through the autonomous imagination of the children: the incongruity between the piety of the shouters and the violence with which the religious gestures of one threatens the minister. Briefly, the author records the joining point between the blues and religious tradition: Miss Grace, the good-time woman, is also conducting rituals of transcendence through her barrelhouse blues for those whose uprush of spirit must have an earthly and fleshly source. The agony in religion and the blues is the connecting point: "A stranger to the music could not have made a distinction between the songs sung a few minutes before [in church] and those being danced to in the gay house."

Despite Grandmother Henderson's strength, the folk religious tradition leaves her with serious limitations. Her giant stature goes to zero, or almost, in any confrontation with the white Southern community, a startling and humiliating experience for the child worshipper of black adult omnipotence. In addition, there is what Ralph Ellison spoke of as a warmth in the folk communal life "accompanied by an equally personal coldness, kindliness by cruelty, regard by malice." It will be recalled that Ellison saw the negative qualities as being activated "against the member who gestures toward individuality." Maya Angelou dramatizes such an action in Chapter 15, a masterful section. Mrs. Bertha Flowers, the town's black intellectual, has ministered to Maya's ever-burgeoning hunger and quest for individuality by giving her a book of poetry, talking to her philosophically about life, and encouraging her to recite poems. Returning to Grandmother Henderson, she happens to say "by the way—." Grandmother gives her a severe beating for using the expression, much to the bewilderment of the child. Later, Grandmother explained that "Jesus was the Way, the Truth and the Light," that "by the way" is really saying "by Jesus," or "by God," and she had no intention of allowing the

Lord's name to be taken in vain in her house. In *Gather Together* Grandmother Henderson gives her a severe, protective beating because Maya had endangered her life by responding to whites' abuse of her in the local clothing store by superlative abuse of her own. Thus, regarding folk religious tradition and other aspects of community confrontations with existence, the author imposes the illusion of striking a just balance between spiritual beauty and absurdity.

> —George E. Kent, "Maya Angelou's *I Know Why the Caged Bird Sings* and Black Autobiographical Tradition," *Kansas Quarterly* 7, No. 3 (Summer 1975): 75–77

LILIANE K. ARENSBERG ON RACIAL SELF-HATRED

[Liliane K. Arensberg is a former professor at Emory University. In this extract, Arensberg focuses on the opening of *I Know Why the Caged Bird Sings* and studies the racial self-hatred it seems to embody.]

Angelou introduces *I Know Why the Caged Bird Sings* with an anecdote. It is Easter Sunday at the Colored Methodist Episcopal Church in Stamps. In celebration of the event, Momma has prepared a lavender taffeta dress for Maya. Believing it to be the most beautiful dress she has ever seen, Maya attributes to it magical properties: when worn, the dress will change Maya into the lovely, blond and blue-eyed "sweet little white girl" she actually believes herself to be.

But on Easter morning the dress reveals its depressing actuality: it is "a plain, ugly cut-down from a white woman's once-was-purple throwaway." No Cinderella metamorphosis for Maya; instead, she lives in a "black dream" from which there is no respite. Unlike Christ, whose resurrection from death the church is celebrating, Maya cannot be reborn into another life. Overcome with the impossibility of her white fantasy, she escapes the church "peeing and crying" her way home. Maya must, indeed, lose control of her body and feelings. "It would probably run right back up to my head," she believes, "and my poor head would burst like a dropped watermelon, and all the brains and spit and tongue and eyes would roll all over the place." By letting go of her fantasy—physically manifested by letting go of her bladder—Maya will not "die from a busted head."

But, to "let go," as Erik Erikson observes in *Childhood and Society*, "can turn into an inimical letting loose of destructive forces." For, on this Easter Sunday Maya Angelou comprehends the futility of her wish to become "one of the sweet little white girls who were everybody's dream of what was right with the world." "If growing up is painful for the Southern Black girl," the adult writer concludes, "being aware of her displacement is the rust on the razor that threatens the throat." Although she acknowledges the "unnecessary insult" of her own white fantasy, Angelou nevertheless puts the rust on the razor by her awareness of its insidious and ubiquitous presence.

The form an autobiography takes is as revealing as its style and content. By placing this anecdote before the body of her narrative, Angelou asserts the paradigmatic importance of this particular event on her life. The atemporality of this experience (Maya's age remains unmentioned) coupled with the symbolic setting of Easter Sunday, suggests a personal myth deeply imbedded in Angelou's unconscious. One could, indeed, speculate that this event, introducing Maya Angelou's autobiography, is the "epiphanic moment" of her youth. For this short narrative presents the two dynamic operatives that circumscribe Angelou's self: her blackness and her outcast position.

Immediately striking in the anecdote is Maya's fantastic belief that "I was really white," that "a cruel fairy stepmother, who was understandably jealous of my beauty" had tricked Maya of her Caucasian birthright. The fairy tale imagery employed to depict her creation is characteristic of the imaginative and impressionable girl, but the meaning of her tale cannot be overlooked. For, according to her schema, Maya's identity hinges on the whims of this fairy stepmother. If benevolent, she will transform Maya back into a pretty white girl; if she remains cruel, her spell over Maya will rest unbroken. When her dress does not produce the longed-for results, Maya is forced to contend with her blackness. But if she acknowledges this blackness, Maya must also acknowledge the existence of an arbitrary and malevolent force beyond her control which dictates her personal and racial identity.

As if mourning the death of the lovely white body beyond her possession, Maya describes her dress as sounding "like crepe paper on the back of hearses." Maya's body indeed becomes a symbolic hearse, containing not only her dead dream, but also a life whose very existence is threatened by the whims of a murderous white culture.

Angelou's highly personal confession of racial self-hatred is, unfortunately, not unique in Afro-American experience. Many works of contemporary black novelists and autobiographers— from Ralph Ellison and Imamu Baraka/LeRoi Jones to Richard Wright and Malcolm X—assert that invisibility, violence, alienation and death are part and parcel of growing up black in a white America. Likewise, psychological and sociological studies affirm that the first lesson in living taught the black child is how to ensure his/her survival. "The child must know," write Grier and Cobbs, "that the white world is dangerous and that if he does not understand its rules it may kill him." It is, then, pitifully understandable for Maya to wish herself white, since blackness forebodes annihilation.

—Liliane K. Arensberg, "Death as Metaphor of Self in I Know Why The Caged Bird Sings," CLA Journal 20, No. 2 (December 1976): 278–80

ADAM DAVID MILLER ON *THE HEART OF A WOMAN*

[Adam David Miller is the editor of *Dices or Black Bones: Black Voices of the Seventies* (1970) and has also written a volume of poems, *Forever Afternoon* (1994). In this extract, taken from a review of Maya Angelou's third autobiography, Miller notes how it covers one of the most exciting periods of black history and praises its vibrant narrative.]

Maya Angelou's book, covering as it does the years roughly 1957–1961, is a third installment of her personal saga. The book also covers one of the most exciting periods in recent African and Afro-American history. The beginning of a new awareness of Africa on the part of Negroes. It is the period of the early civil rights marches, of Malcolm X and Dr. Martin Luther King, Jr., of the Egypt of Nasser and the Ghana of Nkrumah, and the murder of the Congo's Patrice Lumumba. It is also the period when Maya tries her wings and learns that she can fly, of her brief but important marriage to a South African freedom fighter, and the period when her *wunderkind* son, Guy Johnson, grows into manhood.

As with all her books *The Heart of a Woman* can be mined for its riches: instruction, insight, humor, wry wit, lore, and fine writing. From this casebook on successful single parenting, we can see the perils a single mother, in this case a black one, faces in bringing up a black male child in our society, where so many things seem bent on preventing him from reaching adulthood. Beyond the brute struggle to provide, there must be the constant watchfulness to insure that the child is not physically maimed or spiritually stunted. Then there is the danger of bringing up a male child by a lone woman, walking the fine line between sensuality and sexuality, the danger of distorting his sexuality. Maya Angelou shows how one woman succeeds in skirting these dangers and comes out safely on the other side.

In her marriage to Make, we see the inherent problems of an Afro-American marrying a traditional African. No way an African-American woman, used to an essentially equal relation with her man, can long submit to the subservient role an African wife is expected to play. She discovers on her visit to a London Afro-Asian conference that educated African women too, were resenting their marital restraints and were beginning to do something about them.

As befits a master story teller, Maya Angelou's book is rich with the tight sketch, the apt portrait, the pithy line. Like Thoreau, she builds from the sentence. Throughout her account of her many experiences, I am constantly arrested when she uses just the right sentence to share some insight or fix some conclusion.

While Maya Angelou does many things in *The Heart of a Woman*, what she keeps constant throughout the book is that it is the account of a black **W-O-M-A-N**'s life. Her experiences with women, her love and respect for them and theirs for her, her niceness and delicacy in dealing with them, from her mother to her friends, even to mere acquaintances, these could provide a model of conduct for any woman to follow.

Few will come away from this look into Maya Angelou's heart without being moved.

—Adam David Miller, [Review of *The Heart of a Woman*], *Black Scholar* 13, Nos. 4 & 5 (Summer 1982): 48–49

SONDRA O'NEALE ON THE NARRATIVE TECHNIQUE OF ANGELOU'S AUTOBIOGRAPHIES

[Sondra O'Neale (b. 1939) is the author of *Jupiter Hammon and the Biblical Beginnings of African American Literature* (1993). In this extract, O'Neale studies the narrative qualities of Maya Angelou's biographies, noting how closely they resemble the techniques of fiction.]

Unlike her poetry, which is a continuation of traditional oral expression in Afro-American literature, Angelou's prose follows classic technique in nonpoetic Western forms. The material in each book while chronologically marking her life is nonetheless arranged in loosely structured plot sequences which are skillfully controlled. In *Caged Bird* the tenuous psyche of a gangly, sensitive, withdrawn child is traumatically jarred by rape, a treacherous act from which neither the reader nor the protagonist has recovered by the book's end. All else is cathartic: her uncles' justified revenge upon the rapist, her years of readjustment in a closed world of speechlessness despite the warm nurturing of her grandmother, her grand-uncle, her beloved brother Bailey, and the Stamps community; a second reunion with her vivacious mother; even her absurdly unlucky pregnancy at the end does not assuage the reader's anticipatory wonder: isn't the act of rape by a trusted adult so assaultive upon an eight-year-old's life that it leaves a wound which can never be healed? Such reader interest in a character's future is the craft from which quality fiction is made. Few autobiographers however have the verve to seize the drama of such a moment, using one specific incident to control the book but with an underlining implication that the incident will not control a life.

The denouement in *Gather Together in My Name* is again sexual: the older, crafty, experienced man lasciviously preying upon the young, vulnerable, and, for all her exposure by that time, naïve woman. While foreshadowing apprehension guided the reader to the central action in the first work, Maya presses the evolvement in *Gather Together* through a limited first-person narrator who seems to know less of the villain's intention than is obvious to the reader. Thrice removed from the action, the reader sees that L. D. Tolbrook is nothing but a slick pimp, that his seductive sexual refusals can only lead to a calamitous end; that his please-turn-these-few-tricks-for-me-baby-so-I-can-get-out-of-an-urgent-jam line is an ancient inducement for susceptible females, but Maya the actor in the tragedy cannot. She is too much in love. Maya, the author, through whose eyes we see a younger, foolish "self," so painstakingly details the girl's descent into the brothel that Black women, all women, have enough vicarious example to avoid the trap. Again, through using the "self" as role model, not only is Maya able to instruct and inspire the reader but the sacrifice of personal disclosure authenticates the autobiography's integral depth.

—Sondra O'Neale, "Reconstruction of the Complete Self: New Images of Black Women in Maya Angelou's Continuing Autobiography," *Black Women Writers (1950–1980): A Critical Evaluation,* ed. Mari Evans (New York: Anchor Books/Double-day, 1984), pp. 32–33

LUCINDA H. MACKETHAN ON THE DEVELOPMENT OF ANGELOU'S USE OF LANGUAGE

[Lucinda H. Mackethan (b. 1945) has written *The Dream of Arcady: Time and Place in Southern Literature* (1980) and *Daughters of Time: Creating Woman's Voice in Southern Story* (1990). In this extract, Mackethan examines the "word-bringers" (her mother, brother, and other individuals) who nurtured Angelou's early interest in the power of language.]

Angelou the autobiographer takes her childhood self, who goes by many names, on a kind of quest for a name and for words. The book's first scene is comic as well as pathetic: in the Colored Methodist Episcopal Church, young Margeurite Johnson cannot call up the words she is supposed to say in the Easter pageant; at the scene's end, she runs from the church, looking (to herself) a ridiculous figure in lavender taffeta, wetting her pants, laughing to be free from the agonizing turmoil of having to depend on the words of others. The progress of this girl's life is made possible by a series of word-bringers—her brother, her teachers, her mother's con men friends, her mother herself—who gradually open to her the potential of language; words alone can free her from her fear of and dependency on others' conceptions. Thus, with no ability to raise the words she needs, Margeurite in the first scene is betrayed by the white world's view of beauty: "Because I was really white," she tries to think, "and because a cruel fairy stepmother, who was understandably jealous of my beauty, had turned me into a too-big Negro girl, with nappy black hair, broad feet, and a space between her teeth that would hold a number-two pencil." By the end of the book, Maya is not only talking but she has an edge on her white school mates; she and her friends "were alert to the gap separating the written word from the colloquial. We learned to slide out of one language and into another without being conscious of the effort."

The most important of the word-bringers in Maya's life is her mother—a savvy, sassy, street-wise Mama who makes Black beautiful and language a gift of the body as well as an art of the mind. Vivian Baxter Johnson can dance, can shoot a crooked business partner, can make her living in the tough blues joints of St. Louis and San Francisco. Yet most of all she can talk, and unlike Maya's conservative southern grandmother's, her talk is full of hope, irreverence for tradition, and scorn for anyone who thinks they can keep her down. When she repeats the old report, "They tell me the whitefolks still in the lead," she says it, Angelou tells us, "as if that was not quite the whole truth." Vivian's words are a compendium of mother wit: "She had a store of aphorisms," Angelou remarks, "which she dished out as the occasion demanded": "The Man upstairs, He don't make mistakes"; "It ain't no trouble when you pack double"; "Nothing beats a trial but a failure"; and perhaps most to our point, "Sympathy is next to shit in the dictionary, and I can't even read."

While we are given no explicit statement at the end of her story that Margeurite Johnson has fully absorbed what she needs of her mother's verbal capacities, Maya's own nascent motherhood, and her attitude toward becoming a mother, indicate that a survivor is coming into being. She tells us her feelings as a young, unwed mother who managed to hide her pregnancy from her family for almost eight months, and her words have a kind of triumph in them: "I had a baby. He was beautiful and mine. Totally mine. No one had bought him for me. No one had helped me endure the sickly gray months. I had had help in the child's conception, but no one could deny that I had had an immaculate pregnancy." Gone is the girl who could see her Blackness only as some cruel fairy godmother's revenge. With a real mother, and mother wit, Maya has the preparation she needs to become the writer, and word-bringer, who created *I Know Why the Caged Bird Sings.*

—Lucinda H. Mackethan, "Mother Wit: Humor in Afro-American Women's Autobiography," *Studies in American Humor* 4, Nos. 1 & 2 (Spring–Summer 1985): 59–60

KENETH KINNAMON ON ANGELOU'S CELEBRATION OF BLACK CULTURE

[Keneth Kinnamon (b. 1932), a professor of English at the University of Illinois, is a leading critic of black American literature. He is the author of *The Emergence of Richard Wright* (1972) and the editor of *New Essays on Native Son* (1990) and *Conversations with Richard Wright* (1993). In this extract, Kinnamon compares *I Know Why the Caged Bird Sings* with Richard Wright's *Black Boy,* finding in Angelou's work a celebration of black culture absent from Wright's.]

I Know Why the Caged Bird Sings is a celebration of black culture, by no means uncritical, but essentially a celebration. Toward her family, young Marguerite is depicted as loving, whether or not her love is merited. She idolizes her slightly older brother Bailey. Her Grandmother Henderson is presented not only as the matrifocal center of her family but as the leader of the black community in Stamps, strong, competent, religious, skilled in her ability to coexist with Jim Crow while maintaining her personal dignity. She is a repository of racial values, and her store is the secular center of her community. Crippled Uncle Willie could have been presented as a Sherwood Anderson grotesque, but Angelou recalls feeling close to him even if he was, like Grandmother Henderson, a stern disciplinarian. Angelou would seem to have every reason to share Wright's bitterness about parental neglect, but she does not. When her father shows up in Stamps she is impressed by his appearance, his proper speech, and his city ways. Her mother beggars description: "To describe my mother would be to write about a hurricane in its perfect power. Or the climbing, falling colors of a rainbow. . . . My mother's beauty literally assailed me." Absorbed in their own separate lives, her parents neglect or reject her repeatedly, but she is more awed by their persons and their personalities than she is resentful. Her maternal family in St. Louis is also impressive in its worldly way, so different in its emphasis on pleasure and politics from the religious rectitude of the paternal family in Stamps. Even Mr. Freeman, her mother's live-in boyfriend who first abuses and then rapes the child, is presented with more compassion than rancor.

Afflicted with guilt after Freeman is killed by her uncles, Marguerite lapses into an almost catatonic silence, providing an excuse to her mother to send her back to Stamps. Southern passivity provides a good therapeutic environment for the child, especially when she is taken under the wing of an elegant, intelligent black woman named Mrs. Bertha Flowers, who treats her to cookies, Dickens, and good advice. Better dressed and better read than anyone else in the community, she nevertheless maintains good relations with all and urges Marguerite not to neglect the wisdom of the folk as she pursues literary interests: "She said that I must always be intolerant of ignorance but understanding of illiteracy. That some people, unable to go to school, were more educated and even more intelligent than college professors. She encouraged me to listen carefully to what country people called mother wit. That in those homely sayings was couched the collective wisdom of generations." In contrast to Wright's grandmother, who banished from her house the schoolteacher Ella for telling the story of Bluebeard to Richard, Grandmother Henderson is quite friendly with "Sister" Flowers, both women secure in their sense of self and their mutual respect.

Angelou also recalls favorably the larger rituals of black community. Religious exercises, whether in a church or in a tent revival meeting, provide a festive atmosphere for Marguerite and Bailey. Racial euphoria pervades the black quarter of Stamps after a Joe Louis victory in a prizefight broadcast on Uncle Willie's radio to a crowd crammed into the store. A summer fish fry, the delicious feeling of terror while listening to ghost stories, the excitement of pre-graduation activities—these are some of the pleasures of growing up black so amply present in *I Know Why the Caged Bird Sings* and so conspicuously absent in *Black Boy*.

—Keneth Kinnamon, "Call and Response: Intertextuality in Two Autobiographical Works by Richard Wright and Maya Angelou," *Studies in Black American Literature, Volume II: Belief vs. Theory in Black American Literary Criticism,* ed. Joe Weixlmann and Chester J. Fontenot (Greenwood, FL: Penkevill Publishing Co., 1986), pp. 130–31

[Christine Froula (b. 1950) has written *A Guide to Ezra Pound's* Selected Poems (1983) and *To Write Paradise: Style and Error in Pound's* Cantos (1984). In this extract, Froula studies Angelou's rape by her mother's lover at the age of eight and its traumatic aftermath.]

Early in her memoir, Angelou presents a brief but rich *biographia literaria* in the form of a childhood romance: "During these years in Stamps, I met and fell in love with William Shakespeare. He was my first white love. Although I enjoyed and respected Kipling, Poe, Butler, Thackeray and Henley, I saved my young and loyal passion for Paul Lawrence Dunbar, Langston Hughes, James Weldon Johnson and W. E. B. Du Bois' 'Litany at Atlanta.' But it was Shakespeare who said, 'When in disgrace with fortune and men's eyes.' It was a state with which I felt myself most familiar. I pacified myself about his whiteness by saying that after all he had been dead so long that it couldn't matter to anyone any more." Maya and her brother Bailey reluctantly abandon their plan to memorize a scene from Shakespeare—"we realized that Momma would question us about the author and that we'd have to tell her that Shakespeare was white, and it wouldn't matter to her whether he was dead or not"—and choose Johnson's "The Creation" instead. This passage, depicting the trials attending those inter-racial affairs of the mind that Maya must keep hidden from her vigilant grandmother, raises the question of what it means for a female reader and fledgling writer to carry on a love affair with Shakespeare or with male authors in general. While the text overtly confronts and disarms the issue of race, the seduction issue is only glancingly acknowledged. But this literary father-daughter romance resonates quietly alongside Angelou's more disturbing account of the quasi-incestuous rape of the eight-year-old Maya by her mother's lover, Mr. Freeman—particularly by virtue of the line she finds so sympathetic in Shakespeare, "When in disgrace with fortune and men's eyes."

Mr. Freeman's abuse of Maya occurs in two episodes. In the first, her mother rescues her from a nightmare by taking her into her own bed, and Maya then wakes to find her mother gone to work and Mr. Freeman grasping her tightly. The child feels, first, bewilderment and terror: "His right hand was moving so fast and his heart was beating so hard that I was afraid that he would die." When Mr. Freeman subsides, however, so does Maya's fright: "Finally he was quiet, and then came the nice part. He held me so softly that I wished he wouldn't ever let me go. . . . This was probably my real father and we had found each other at last." After the abuse comes the silencing: Mr. Freeman enlists the child's complicity by an act of metaphysical violence, informing her that he will kill her beloved brother Bailey if she tells anyone what "they" have done. For the child, this prohibition prevents not so much telling as asking, for, confused as she is by her conflicting feelings, she has no idea what has happened. One day, however, Mr. Freeman stops her as she is setting out for the library, and it is then that he commits the actual rape on the terrified child, "a breaking and entering when even the senses are torn apart." Again threatened with violence if she tells, Maya retreats to her bed in a silent delirium, but the story emerges when her mother discovers her stained drawers, and Mr. Freeman is duly arrested and brought to trial.

At the trial, the defense lawyer as usual attempts to blame the victim for her own rape. When she cannot remember what Mr. Freeman was wearing, "he snickered as though I had raped Mr. Freeman." His next question, as to whether Mr. Freeman had ever touched her prior to that Saturday, reduces her to confusion because her memory of her own pleasure in being held by him seems to her to implicate her in his crime: "I couldn't say yes and tell them how he had loved me once for a few minutes and how he had held me close. . . . My uncles would kill me and Grandmother Baxter would stop speaking. . . . And all those people in the court would stone me as they had stoned the harlot in the Bible. And mother, who thought I was such a good girl, would be so disappointed." An adult can see that the daughter's need for a father's affection does not cancel his culpability for sexually abusing her. But the child cannot resolve the conflict between her desire to tell the truth, which means acknowledging the pleasure she felt when Mr. Freeman gently held her, and her awareness of the social condemnation that would greet this revelation. She knows the cultural script and its hermeneutic traditions, which hold all female pleasure guilty, all too well, and so she betrays her actual experience with a lie: "Everyone in the court knew that the answer had to be No. Everyone except Mr. Freeman and me. . . . I said No." But she chokes on the lie and has to be taken down from the stand. Mr. Freeman is sentenced to a year and a day, but somehow manages to be released that very afternoon; and not long thereafter, he is killed by her Baxter uncles. Hearing of Mr. Freeman's death, Maya is overwhelmed with terror and remorse: "A man was dead because I lied." Taking his death as proof that her words have power to kill, she descends into a silence that lasts for a year. Like Helen's sacrificial speech, Maya's silence speaks the hysterical cultural script: it expresses guilt and anguish at her own aggression against the father and voluntarily sacrifices the cure of truthful words.

—Christine Froula, "The Daughter's Seduction: Sexual Violence and Literary History," *Signs: Journal of Women in Culture and Society* 11, No. 4 (Summer 1986): 634–35

MARY JANE LUPTON ON MOTHERHOOD IN ANGELOU'S AUTOBIOGRAPHIES

[Mary Jane Lupton is a professor of English at Morgan State University. She is the coauthor of *The Curse: A Cultural History of Menstruation* (1976) and the author of *Menstruation and Psychoanalysis* (1993). In this extract, Lupton finds motherhood a dominant theme in Angelou's otherwise open-ended autobiographies.]

What distinguishes, then, Angelou's autobiographical method from more conventional autobiographical forms is her very denial of closure. The reader of autobiography expects a beginning, a middle, and an end—as occurs in *Caged Bird*. She or he also expects a central experience, as we indeed are given in the extraordinary rape sequence of *Caged Bird*. But Angelou, by continuing her narrative, denies the form and its history, creating from each ending a new beginning, relocating the center to some luminous place in a volume yet to be.

Stretching the autobiographical canvas, she moves forward: from being a child; to being a mother; to leaving the child; to having the child, in the fifth volume, achieve his independence. Nor would I be so unwise as to call the fifth volume the end. For Maya Angelou, now a grandmother, has already published a moving, first-person account in *Woman's Day* of the four years of anguish surrounding the maternal kidnapping of her grandson Colin.

Throughout the more episodic volumes, the theme of motherhood remains a unifying element, with Momma Henderson being Angelou's link with the Black folk tradition—as George Kent, Elizabeth Schultz, and other critics have mentioned. Since traditional solidity of development is absent, one must sometimes search through three or four books to trace Vivian Baxter's changing lovers, Maya Angelou's ambivalence towards motherhood, or her son Guy's various reactions to his non-traditional upbringing. Nonetheless, the volumes are intricately related through a number of essential elements: the ambivalent autobiographical voice, the flexibility of structure to echo the life process, the intertextual commentary on character and theme, and the use of certain recurring patterns to establish both continuity and continuation. I have isolated the mother-child pattern as a way of approaching the complexity of Angelou's methods. One could as well select other kinds of interconnected themes: the absent and/or substitute father, the use of food as a psycho-sexual symbol, the dramatic/symbolic use of images of staring or gazing, and other motifs which establish continuity within and among the volumes.

Stephen Butterfield says of *Caged Bird:* "Continuity is achieved by the contact of mother and child, the sense of life begetting life that happens automatically in spite of all confusion—perhaps also because of it." The consistent yet changing connection for Maya Angelou through the four subsequent narratives is that same contact of mother and child—with herself and her son Guy; with herself and her own mother, Vivian Baxter; with herself and her paternal grandmother; and, finally, with the child-mother in herself.

Moreover, in extending the traditional one-volume form, Angelou has metaphorically mothered another book. The "sense of life begetting life" at the end of *Caged Bird* can no longer signal the conclusion of the narrative. The autobiographical moment has been reopened and expanded; Guy's birth can now be seen symbolically as the birth of another text. In a 1975 interview with Carol Benson, Angelou uses such a birthing metaphor in describing the writing of *Gather Together:* "If you have a child, it takes nine months. It took me three-and-a-half years to write *Gather Together,* so I couldn't just drop it." This statement makes emphatic what in the autobiographies are much more elusive comparisons between creative work and motherhood; after a three-and-a-half-year pregnancy she gives birth to *Gather Together,* indicating that she must have planned the conception of the second volume shortly after the 1970 delivery of *Caged Bird.*

Each of the five volumes explores, both literally and metaphorically, the significance of motherhood. I will examine this theme from two specific perspectives: first, Angelou's relationship to her mother and to mother substitutes, especially to Momma Henderson; second, Angelou's relationship to her son as she struggles to define her own role as mother/artist. Throughout the volumes Angelou moves backwards and forwards, from connection to conflict. This dialectic of Black mother-daughterhood, introduced in the childhood narrative, enlarges and contracts during the series, finding its fullest expression in *Singin' and Swingin' and Gettin' Merry Like Christmas.*

> —Mary Jane Lupton, "Singing the Black Mother: Maya Angelou and Autobiographical Continuity," *Black American Literature Forum* 24, No. 2 (Summer 1990): 258–60

CAROL E. NEUBAUER ON ANGELOU'S RELATIONSHIP WITH HER MOTHER

[Carol E. Neubauer teaches English and American literature at Bradley University. In this extract, Neubauer examines Angelou's relationship with her mother and its role in combating a sense of displacement in her life.]

In *Caged Bird,* Angelou recounts many explosive incidents of the racial discrimination she experienced as a child. In the 1930s, Stamps was a fully segregated town. Marguerite and Bailey, however, are welcomed by a grandmother who is not only devoted to them but, as owner of the Wm. Johnson General Merchandise Store, is highly successful and independent. Momma is their most constant source of love and strength. "I saw only her power and strength. She was taller than any woman in my personal world, and her hands were so large they could span my head from ear to ear." As powerful as her grandmother's presence seems to Marguerite, Momma uses her strength solely to guide and protect her family but not to confront the white community directly. Momma's resilient power usually reassures Marguerite, but one of the child's most difficult lessons teaches her that racial prejudice in Stamps can effectively circumscribe and even defeat her grandmother's protective influence.

In fact, it is only in the autobiographical narrative that Momma's personality begins to loom larger than life and provides Angelou's memories of childhood with a sense of personal dignity and meaning. On one occasion, for example, Momma takes Marguerite to the local dentist to be treated for a severe toothache. The dentist, who is ironically named Lincoln, refuses to treat the child, even though he is indebted to Momma for a loan she extended to him during the depression: " 'Annie, my policy is I'd rather stick my hand in a dog's mouth than in a nigger's.' " As a silent witness to this scene, Marguerite suffers not only from the pain of her two decayed teeth, which have been reduced to tiny enamel bits by the avenging "Angel of the candy counter," but also from the utter humiliation of the dentist's bigotry as well: "It seemed terribly unfair to have a toothache and a headache and have to bear at the same time the heavy burden of Blackness."

In an alternate version of the confrontation, which Angelou deliberately fantasizes and then italicizes to emphasize its invention, Momma asks Marguerite to wait for her outside the dentist's office. As the door closes, the frightened child imagines her grandmother becoming "ten feet tall with eight-foot arms." Without mincing words, Momma instructs Lincoln to " 'leave Stamps by sundown' " and " 'never again practice dentistry' " : " 'When you get settled in your next place, you will be a vegetarian caring for dogs with the mange, cats with the cholera and cows with the epizootic. Is that clear?' " The poetic justice in Momma's superhuman power is perfect; the racist dentist who refused to treat her ailing granddaughter will in the future be restricted to treating the dogs he prefers to "niggers." After a trip to the black dentist in Texarkana, Momma and Marguerite return to Stamps, where we learn the "real" version of the story by overhearing a conversation between Momma and Uncle Willie. In spite of her prodigious powers, all that Momma accomplishes in Dr. Lincoln's office is to demand ten dollars as unpaid interest on the loan to pay for their bus trip to Texarkana.

In the child's imagined version, fantasy comes into play as the recounted scene ventures into the unreal or the impossible. Momma becomes a sort of superwoman of enormous proportions ("ten feet tall with eight-foot arms") and comes to the helpless child's rescue. In this alternate vision, Angelou switches to fantasy to suggest the depth of the child's humiliation and the residue of pain even after her two bad teeth have been pulled. Fantasy, finally, is used to demonstrate the undiminished strength of the character of Momma. Summarizing the complete anecdote, Angelou attests, "I preferred, much preferred, my version." Carefully selected elements of fiction and fantasy in the scene involving Dr. Lincoln and her childhood hero, Momma, partially compensate for the racial displacement that she experiences as a child.

When Angelou is thirteen, she and Bailey leave the repressive atmosphere of Stamps to join their mother. During these years, she continues to look for a place in life that will dissolve her sense of displacement. By the time she and Bailey are in their early teens, they have crisscrossed the western half of the country traveling between their parents' separate homes and their grandmother's in Stamps. Her sense of geographic displacement alone would be enough to upset any child's security, since the life-styles of her father in southern California and her mother in St. Louis and later in San Francisco represent worlds completely different and even foreign to the pace of life in the rural South. Each time the children move, a different set of relatives or another of their parents' lovers greets them, and they never feel a part of a stable family group, except when they are in Stamps at the general store with Momma and Uncle Willie.

Once settled in San Francisco in the early 1940s, Angelou enrolls at George Washington High School and the California Labor School, where she studies dance and drama in evening classes. She excels in both schools, and her teachers quickly recognize her intelligence and talent. Later she breaks the color barrier by becoming the first black female conductor on the San Francisco streetcars. Just months before her high school graduation, she engages in a onetime sexual encounter to prove her sexuality to herself and becomes pregnant. *Caged Bird,* however, ends on a note of awakening with the birth of her son and the beginning of a significant measure of strength and confidence in her ability to succeed and find her place in life. As autobiographer, Angelou uses the theme of displacement to unify the first volume of her life story as well as to suggest her long-term determination to create security and permanency in her life.

—Carol E. Neubauer, "Maya Angelou: Self and a Song of Freedom in the Southern Tradition," *Southern Women Writers: The New Generation,* ed. Tonette Bond Inge (Tuscaloosa: University of Alabama Press, 1990), pp. 117–19

DOLLY A. MCPHERSON ON THE IMPORTANCE OF ANGELOU'S AUTOBIOGRAPHICAL WORKS

[Dolly A. McPherson is a professor of English at Wake Forest University and the author of *Order out of Chaos: The Autobiographical Works of Maya Angelou* (1990), from which the following extract is taken. Here,

McPherson stresses the importance of Angelou's autobiographies in the insights it offers into black culture.]

Through the genre of autobiography, Angelou has celebrated the richness and vitality of Southern Black life and the sense of community that persists in the face of poverty and racial prejudice, initially revealing this celebration through a portrait of life as experienced by a Black child in the Arkansas of the 1930s (*I Know Why the Caged Bird Sings*, 1969). The second delineates a young woman struggling to create an existence that provides security and love in post–World War II America (*Gather Together in My Name*, 1974). The third presents a young, married adult in the 1950s seeking a career in show business and experiencing her first amiable contacts with Whites (*Singin' and Swingin' and Gettin' Merry Like Christmas*, 1976). The fourth volume (*The Heart of a Woman*, 1981) shows a wiser, more mature woman in the 1960s, examining the roles of being a woman and a mother. In her most recent volume, Angelou demonstrates that *All God's Children Need Traveling Shoes* (1986) to take them beyond familiar borders and to enable them to see and understand the world from another's vantage point.

While the burden of this serial autobiography is essentially a recapturing of her own subjective experiences, Angelou's effort throughout her work is to describe the influences—personal as well as cultural, historical and social—that have shaped her life. Dominant in Angelou's autobiography is the exploration of the self—the self in relationship with intimate others: the family, the community, the world. Angelou does not recount these experiences simply because they occurred, but because they represent stages of her spiritual growth and awareness—what one writer calls "stages of self." ⟨. . .⟩

A study of Maya Angelou's autobiography is significant not only because the autobiography offers insights into personal and group experience in America, but because it creates a unique place within Black autobiographical tradition, not because it is better than its formidable autobiographical predecessors, but because Angelou, throughout her autobiographical writing, adopts a special stance in relation to the self, the community and the world. Angelou's concerns with family and community, as well as with work and her conceptions of herself as a human being, are echoed throughout her autobiography. The ways in which she faces these concerns offer instruction into the range of survival strategies available to women in America and reveal, as well, important insights into Black traditions and culture.

—Dolly A. McPherson, Order out of Chaos: The Autobiographical Works of Maya Angelou (New York: Peter Lang, 1990), pp. 5–6

Mary Vermillion on Rape and Self-Expression

[Mary Vermillion teaches at the University of Iowa. In this extract, Vermillion studies Angelou's rape and the devastating effects it had on her capacity for self-expression.]

Rape in Angelou's text, however, primarily represents the black girl's difficulties in controlling, understanding, and respecting both her body and her words in a somatophobic society that sees "sweet little white girls" as "everybody's dream of what was right with the world." Angelou connects white definitions of beauty with rape by linking Maya's rape with her first sight of her mother, Vivian Baxter. Angelou's description of Vivian echoes that of the ghost-like whites who baffle young Maya. Vivian has "even white teeth and her fresh-butter color looked see-through clean." Maya and her brother, Bailey, later determine that Vivian resembles a white movie star. Angelou writes that her mother's beauty "literally assailed" Maya and twice observes that she was "struck dumb." This assault by her mother's beauty anticipates the physical assault by Mr. Freeman, her mother's boyfriend, and Maya's muteness upon meeting her mother foreshadows her silence after the rape. With this parallel Angelou indicates that both rape and the dominant white culture's definitions of beauty disempower the black woman's body and self-expression.

Angelou further demonstrates the intimate connection between the violation of Maya's body and the devaluation of her words by depicting her self-imposed silence after Freeman's rape trial. Freeman's pleading looks in the courtroom, along with Maya's own shame, compel her to lie, and after she learns that her uncles have murdered Freeman, she believes that her courtroom lie is responsible for his death. Angelou describes the emotions that silence Maya:

> I could feel the evilness flowing through my body and waiting, pent up, to rush off my tongue if I tried to open my mouth. I clamped my teeth shut, I'd hold it in. If it escaped, wouldn't it flood the world and all the innocent people?

Angelou's use of flood imagery in this crucial passage enables her to link Maya's inability to control her body and her words. Throughout the text Maya's failure to keep her bodily functions "pent up" signals the domination of her body by others. The autobiography's opening scene merges her inability to control her appearance, words, and bodily functions. Wanting to look like a "sweet little white girl," Maya is embarrassed about her own appearance and cannot remember the words of the Easter poem she recites. With her escape from the church, Angelou implicitly associates Maya's inability to rule her bladder with her inability to speak:

> I stumbled and started to say something, or maybe to scream, but a green persimmon, or it could have been a lemon, caught me between the legs and squeezed. I tasted the sour on my tongue and felt it in the back of my mouth. Then before I reached the door, the sting was burning down my legs and into my Sunday socks. I tried to hold, to squeeze it back, to keep it from speeding.

Maya's squeezing back in this passage anticipates her stopping the flood of her words after the rape, and Angelou also connects this opening scene of urination with one of Freeman's means of silencing Maya. After ejaculating on a mattress, he tells her that she has wet the bed, and with this lie, he denies her knowledge about her own body and confounds her ability to make a coherent story out of his actions.

This inability to create a story about her body pervades the remainder of *Caged Bird* as Maya struggles to cope with her emerging womanhood. Angelou, however, is not content to let the mute, sexually abused, wishing-to-be-white Maya represent the black female body in her text. Instead, she begins to reembody Maya by critiquing her admiration for white literary discourse. An early point at which Angelou foregrounds this critique is in Maya's meeting with Mrs. Bertha, Flowers. Presenting this older black woman as the direct opposite of young Maya, Angelou stresses that Flowers magnificently rules both her words and her body. Indeed Flowers's bodily control seems almost supernatural: "She had the grace of control to appear warm in the coldest weather, and on the Arkansas summer days it seemed she had a private breeze which swirled around, cooling her." She makes Maya proud to be black, and Maya claims that Flowers is more beautiful and "just as refined as whitefolks in movies and books." Although Maya begins to respect and admire the black female body, white heroines still provide her standard for beauty, and Angelou pokes fun at the literary discourse that whitens Maya's view of Bertha Flowers and womanhood:

> She [Flowers] appealed to me because she was like people I had never met personally. Like women in English novels who walked the moors (whatever they were) with their loyal dogs racing at a respectful distance. Like the women who sat in front of roaring fireplaces, drinking tea incessantly from silver trays full of scones and crumpets. Women who walked over the 'heath' and read morocco-bound books.

This humorous passage demonstrates that Maya's self-perception remains dangerously regulated by white culture. Angelou treats such regulation less comically when Flowers breaks Maya's self-imposed silence by asking her to read aloud. The first words Maya speaks after her long spell of muteness are those of Charles Dickens.

Angelou dramatizes the danger that a borrowed voice poses to Maya in her description of Maya's relationship with Viola Cullinan. Maya makes fun of this white woman, whose kitchen she briefly works in, until she discovers that Cullinan's husband has two daughters by a black woman. Then Maya—in a gesture of sisterhood and empathy that is never returned by Cullinan— pities her employer and decides to write a "tragic ballad" "on being white, fat, old and without children." Such a ballad would, of course, completely exclude Maya's own experience: black, thin, young, and (near the end of her autobiography) with child. Through Maya's speculation that Cullinan walks around with no organs and drinks alcohol to keep herself "embalmed," Angelou implies that Maya's potential poetic identification with Cullinan nearly negates her own body. Cullinan's empty insides echo Maya's own perception of herself after the rape as a "gutless doll" she had earlier ripped to pieces.

—Mary Vermillion, "Reembodying the Self: Representations of Rape in Incidents in the Life of a Slave Girl and I Know Why The Caged Bird Sings," Biography 15, No. 3 (Summer 1992): 251–53

ONITA ESTES-HICKS ON ANGELOU'S DEPARTURE FROM THE SOUTH

[Onita Estes-Hicks is a professor of English at the State University of New York at Old Westbury. In this extract, Estes-Hicks discusses the conflicting emotions Angelou felt at her departure from the South.]

Maya Angelou, in her popular *I Know Why the Caged Bird Sings,* attributes her youthful departure from the South, which served as home to her and her beloved brother Bailey, to their wise grandmother's concern for Bailey's safety after a local white forced Angelou's fourteen-year-old sibling to assist in disposing of the body of a "dead and rotten" black male. While documenting the "forced-flight" pattern of earlier Black South autobiographies and acknowledging the "burden of impotent pain" which Jean Toomer so movingly captured in his autobiographical *Cane,* Angelou was to pay homage to that soulful beauty which Toomer himself had found in the old apartheid South during his brief 1922 sojourn in Sparta, Georgia. Joanne Braxton's study *Black Women Writing Autobiography* calls attention to *Caged Bird*'s radiant remembrances of things past in Stamps, Arkansas, tracing Angelou's vision of nurturing family and cohesive community to post-gyneric influences in the genre of autobiography.

Punctuated by life-sustaining community rituals involving church gatherings, storytelling sessions in the family-owned store, and cooperative work projects (such as annual hog slaughterings, preserving and canning activities, and work in the cotton fields), Angelou's poignant portraits of her immediate family's orderly daily life suggest some measure of the stability which graced the lives of Black Southerners based on the mutual need, reciprocal respect, and shared compassion which oppression encouraged. Maya's grandmother's store, "the lay center of activities in town," gave the writer a Hurston-like post from which to observe the rich life of small-town Arkansas in the thirties during her ten-year stay in the South:

> In those tender mornings the Store was full of laughing, joking, boasting and bragging. One man was going to pick two hundred pounds of cotton, and another three hundred. Even the children were promising to bring home fo' bits and six bits.

—Onita Estes-Hicks, "The Way We Were: Precious Memories of the Black Segregated South," *African American Review* 27, No. 1 (Spring 1993): 11

JAMES BERTOLINO ON ANGELOU'S HONESTY

[James Bertolino (b. 1942), a prolific poet and critic, has been a professor of English at Skagit Valley College and the University of Cincinnati. In this extract, Bertolino praises the honesty with which *I Know Why the Caged Bird Sings* is written, especially in its straightforward and unsensationalized accounts of traumatic events in Angelou's life.]

What is perhaps most distinctive about Maya Angelou's writing is its consummate felicity. She not only writes with unflinching honesty about her most painful moments, she crafts language that will enact the reality: you feel the textures, smell the odors, shiver with the chill of stunned awareness.

While she was recognized early as a gifted child, she was physically different from her peers as well. Tall and skinny, by age sixteen she was six feet with a body "shaped like a cucumber." Her parents were both beautiful and, at least in her father's case, quite vain. Her only brother, Bailey (a year older), whom she treasured above all else, was also a beautiful child. "Where I was big, elbowy and grating, he was small, graceful and smooth. . . . His hair fell down in black curls, and my head was covered with black steel wool."

As a young child Maya, or Marguerite, was so unhappy about her appearance she fantasized a personal myth: ". . . a cruel fairy stepmother, who was understandably jealous of my beauty, had turned me into a too-big Negro girl, with nappy black hair, broad feet and a space between her teeth that would hold a number-two pencil." As she approached her teens, her Uncle Tommy often told her, ". . . don't worry 'cause you ain't pretty. Plenty pretty women I seen digging ditches or worse. You smart. I swear to God, I rather you have a good mind than a cute behind."

Her personal development did become focussed on her mental abilities, and her creative talents. She apparently was wise enough to take her uncle's advice, though as she matured she also managed to turn her physical limitations to her advantage. She trained her deep, theatrical voice, took dance lessons, and became well-known for her commanding presence on the stage and, later, television.

A key event in her development was being taken in as a protege by a Mrs. Flowers, the only black woman in Stamps with aristocratic bearing. She encouraged Maya to memorize and recite poetry, insisting that ". . . words mean more than what is set down on paper. It takes a human voice to infuse them with the shades of deeper meaning." Maya was about nine years old at the time, and had already suffered through an intense emotional period when she would not, or could not, speak— a reaction to having been molested and raped when she was eight. ⟨. . .⟩

Angelou's description of her molestation and rape is probably the most valuable part of her remarkable book. We live in a time when the issue of child abuse has almost become an obsession in our society, and it's important that such a story be told honestly, without sensationalism, yet with enough palpable detail and enough insight so we, the readers, might begin to understand. Her language resonates with the New Testament at the same time it strikes us with its psychological insight and stark details: "A breaking and entering when even the senses are torn apart. The act of rape on an eight-year-old body is a matter of the needle giving because the camel can't. The child gives, because the body can, and the mind of the violator cannot."

Mr. Freeman was convicted of his crime; however, his lawyer got him released on some technicality, and before the day was over Mr. Freeman was dead. The policeman who delivered the news said it looked like he'd been kicked to death (probably by Maya's uncles, though the responsible parties were never found). For many years Maya felt guilt and remorse over Mr. Freeman's death, for the fact that her words had convinced the court. For though he'd ravaged her horribly, he'd nonetheless been the closest thing she'd had to a real father. And though Mr. Freeman "had surely done something very wrong . . . I was convinced that I had helped him do it."

—James Bertolino, "Maya Angelou Is Three Writers: *I Know Why the Caged Bird Sings,*" *Censored Books: Critical Viewpoints,* ed. Nicholas J. Karolides, Lee Burress, and John M. Kean (Metuchen, NJ: Scarecrow Press, 1993), pp. 300–302

OPAL MOORE ON OPPOSITION TO *I KNOW WHY THE CAGED BIRD SINGS*

[Opal Moore is a professor of English at Radford University. In this extract, Moore argues that opposition to the teaching of *I Know Why the Caged Bird*

Sings in schools is based upon a misunderstanding of the purposes behind its discussion of "adult" themes.]

I Know Why the Caged Bird Sings, the autobiography of Maya Angelou, is the story of one girl's growing up. But, like any literary masterpiece, the story of this one black girl declaring "I can" to a color-coded society that in innumerable ways had told her "you can't, you won't" transcends its author. It is an affirmation; it promises that life, if we have the courage to live it, will be worth the struggle. A book of this description might seem good reading for junior high and high school students. According to People for the American Way, however, *Caged Bird* was the ninth "most frequently challenged book" in American schools. *Caged Bird* elicits criticism for its honest depiction of rape, its exploration of the ugly spectre of racism in America, its recounting of the circumstances of Angelou's own out-of-wedlock teen pregnancy, and its humorous poking at the foibles of the institutional church. Arguments advocating that *Caged Bird* be banned from school reading lists reveal that the complainants, often parents, tend to regard any treatment of these kinds of subject matter in school as inappropriate—despite the fact that the realities and issues of sexuality and violence, in particular, are commonplace in contemporary teenage intercourse and discourse. The children, they imply, are too innocent for such depictions; they might be harmed by the truth.

This is a curious notion—that seriousness should be banned from the classroom while beyond the classroom, the irresponsible and sensational exploitation of sexual, violent, and profane materials is as routine as the daily dose of soap opera. The degradation of feeling caused by slurs directed against persons for their race/class/sex/sexual preference is one of the more difficult hurdles of youthful rites of passage. But it's not just bad TV or the meanness of children. More and more, society is serving an unappetizing fare on a child-sized plate—television screens, t-shirt sloganeers, and weak politicians admonish children to "say 'no' to drugs and drugpushers"; to be wary of strangers; to have safe sex; to report their own or other abusing parents, relatives or neighbors; to be wary of friends; to recognize the signs of alcoholism; to exercise self control in the absence of parental or societal controls; even to take their Halloween candy to the hospital to be x-rayed before consumption. In response to these complications in the landscape of childhood, parent groups, religious groups, and media have called for educators to "bring morality back into the classroom" while we "get back to basics" in a pristine atmosphere of moral non-complexity, outside of the context of the very real world that is squeezing in on that highly touted childhood innocence every single day.

Our teenagers are inundated with the discouragements of life. Ensconced in a literal world, they are shaping their life choices within the dichotomies of TV ads: Bud Light vs. "A mind is a terrible thing to waste." Life becomes a set of skewed and cynical oppositions: "good" vs. easy; yes vs. "catch me"; "right" vs. expediency.

In truth, what young readers seem most innocent of these days is not sex, murder, or profanity, but concepts of self empowerment, faith, struggle as quest, the nobility of intellectual inquiry, survival, and the nature and complexity of moral choice. *Caged Bird* offers these seemingly abstract (adult) concepts to a younger audience that needs to know that their lives are not inherited or predestined, that they can be participants in an exuberant struggle to subjugate traditions of ignorance and fear. Critics of this book might tend to overlook or devalue the necessity of such insights for the young.

Caged Bird's critics imply an immorality in the work based on the book's images. However, it is through Angelou's vivid depictions of human spiritual triumph *set against a backdrop* of human weakness and failing that the autobiography speaks dramatically about moral choice. Angelou paints a picture of some of the negative choices: white America choosing to oppress groups of people; choosing lynch law over justice; choosing intimidation over honor. She offers, however, "deep talk" on the possibility of positive choices: choosing life over death (despite the difficulty of that life); choosing courage over safety; choosing discipline over chaos; choosing voice over silence; choosing compassion over pity, over hatred, over habit; choosing work and planning and hope over useless recrimination and slovenly despair. The book's detractors seem unwilling to admit that morality is not edict (or an innate property of innocence), but the learned capacity for judgement, and that the necessity of moral choice arises only in the presence of the soul's imperfection.

Self empowerment, faith, struggle as quest, survival, intellectual curiosity, complexity of choice—these ideas are the underpinning of Maya Angelou's story. To explore these themes, the autobiography poses its own set of oppositions: Traditional society and values vs. contemporary society and its values; silence vs. self expression; literacy vs. the forces of oppression; the nature of generosity vs. the nature of cruelty; spirituality vs. ritual. Every episode of *Caged Bird,* engages these and other ideas in Maya Angelou's portrait of a young girl's struggle against adversity—a struggle against rape: rape of the body, the soul, the mind, the future, of expectation, of tenderness—towards identity and self affirmation. If we cannot delete rape from our lives, should we delete it from a book about life?

—Opal Moore, "Learning to Live: When the Bird Breaks from the Cage," *Censored Books: Critical Viewpoints,* ed. Nicholas J. Karolides, Lee Burgess, and John M. Kean (Metuchen, NJ: Scarecrow Press, 1993), pp. 306–8

Works by Maya Angelou

I Know Why the Caged Bird Sings. 1969.

Just Give Me a Cool Drink of Water 'fore I Diiie: The Poetry of Maya Angelou. 1971, 1988 (with *Oh Pray My Wings Are Gonna Fit Me Well*).

Gather Together in My Name. 1974, 1985.

Oh Pray My Wings Are Gonna Fit Me Well. 1975.

Singin' and Swingin' and Gettin' Merry Like Christmas. 1976.

And Still I Rise. 1978.

Weekend Glory. 198–.

The Heart of a Woman. 1981.

Shaker, Why Don't You Sing? 1983.

All God's Children Need Traveling Shoes. 1986.

Now Sheba Sings the Songs. 1986.

Conversations with Maya Angelou. Ed. Jeffrey M. Elliot. 1989.

I Shall Not Be Moved. 1990.

On the Pulse of Morning. 1993.

Soul Looks Back in Wonder. 1993.

Lessons in Living. 1993.

Life Doesn't Frighten Me. 1993.

Wouldn't Take Nothing for My Journey Now. 1993.

I Love the Look of Words. 1993.

And My Best Friend Is Chicken. 1994.

Complete Collected Poems. 1994.

My Painted House, My Friendly Chicken, and Me. 1994.

Phenomenal Woman: Four Poems Celebrating Women. 1994.

Our Grandmothers. 1994.

Works about Maya Angelou and I Know Why the Caged Bird Sings

Aldan, Daisy. Review of *The Heart of a Woman. World Literature Today* 56 (1982): 697.

"The *Black Scholar* Interviews: Maya Angelou." *Black Scholar* 8, No. 4 (January–February 1977): 44–53.

Blackburn, Regina. "In Search of the Black Female Self." In *Women's Autobiography: Essays in Criticism,* ed. Estelle C. Jelinek. Bloomington: Indiana University Press, 1980, pp. 133–48.

Cordell, Shirley J. "The Black Woman: A Focus on 'Strength of Character' in *I Know Why the Caged Bird Sings." Virginia English Bulletin* 36, No. 2 (Winter 1986): 36–39.

Cudjoe, Selwyn R. "Maya Angelou and the Autobiographical Statement." In *Black Women Writers (1950–1980): A Critical Evaluation,* ed. Mari Evans. New York: Anchor Books/Doubleday, 1984, pp. 6–24.

Demetrakopoulos, Stephanie A. "The Metaphysics of the Matrilinearism in Women's Autobiography." In *Women's Autobiography,* ed. Estelle C. Jelinek. Bloomington: Indiana University Press, 1980, pp. 180–205.

Elliot, Jeffrey. "Maya Angelou: In Search of Self." *Negro History Bulletin* 40 (1977): 694–95.

Fulghum, Robert. "Home Truths and Homilies." *Washington Post Book World,* 19 September 1993, p. 4.

Georgoudaki, Ekaterini. *Race, Gender, and Class Perspectives in the Works of Maya Angelou, Gwendolyn Brooks, Rita Dove, Nikki Giovanni, and Audre Lorde.* Thessaloniki, Greece: Aristotle University of Thessaloniki, 1991.

Gilbert, Sandra M. "A Platoon of Poets." *Poetry* 128 (1976): 290–99.

Gilbert, Susan. "Maya Angelou's *I Know Why the Caged Bird Sings:* Paths to Escape." *Mount Olive Review* 1, No. 1 (Spring 1987): 39–50.

Grumbach, Doris. "Fine Print." *New Republic,* 6 & 13 July 1974, pp. 30–32.

Hull, Gloria T. "Covering Ground." *Belles Lettres* 6, No. 3 (Spring 1991): 1–2.

Ikerionwu, Maria K. Mootry. "A Black Woman's Story." *Phylon* 44 (1983): 86–87.

Kizer, Carolyn. Review of *Shaker, Why Don't You Sing? Washington Post Book World,* 26 June 1983, p. 8.

Mberi, Antar Sudan Katara. "Like a Cool Glass of Water." *Freedomways* 19, No. 2 (Second Quarter 1979): 109–10.

Megna-Wallace, Joanne. "Simone de Beauvoir and Maya Angelou: Birds of a Feather." *Simone de Beauvoir Studies* 6 (1989): 49–55.

Neubauer, Carol E. "Displacement and Autobiographical Style in Maya Angelou's *The Heart of a Woman.*" *Black American Literature Forum* 17 (1983): 123–29.

Phillips, Frank Lamont. Review of *Gather Together in My Name. Black World* 24, No. 9 (July 1975): 52, 61.

Redmond, Eugene. "Boldness of Language and Breadth: An Interview with Maya Angelou." *Black American Literature Forum* 22 (1988): 156–57.

————. Review of *And Still I Rise! Black Scholar* 8, No. 1 (September 1976): 50–51.

Rosinsky, Natalie N. "Mothers and Daughters: Another Minority Group." In *The Lost Tradition: Mothers and Daughters in Literature,* ed. Cathy N. Davidson and E. M. Brower. New York: Ungar, 1980, pp. 280–90.

Stepto, Robert B. "The Phenomenal Women and the Severed Daughter." *Parnassus: Poetry in Review* 8, No. 1 (Fall–Winter 1979): 312–20.

Tate, Claudia. "Maya Angelou." In Tate's *Black Women Writers at Work.* New York: Continuum, 1983, pp. 1–11.

Index of Themes and Ideas

ALL GOD'S CHILDREN NEED TRAVELING SHOES, and how it compares, 49

ANGELOU, MAYA (MARGUERITE JOHNSON): and the civil rights movement, 7, 34; continuity in works of, 44–45; first exposure to death, 17; as grandmother, 44; honesty of, 27, 36, 54–56; literary style of, 24, 27, 56; marriages of, 7, 34; muteness of, 14, 35–36, 40, 42, 43, 55; name of, 12; narrative technique of, 35–36; pregnancy of, 20–21, 36, 38, 45, 48; at presidential inauguration, 8; as prostitute, 7, 36; reading loved by, 13, 14–15, 22, 30, 41, 55; self-consciousness of, 22, 25–26; sexual doubts of, 20; as streetcar conductor, 7, 20, 48; theatrical experience of, 7, 55

BAILEY, DADDY, and his role in the autobiography, 12, 19, 22, 39

BLACK BOY (Wright), and how it compares, 25–26, 39–40

BODY IMAGE, as theme, 25–26, 31–33, 37, 50–53, 55

CANE (Toomer), and how it compares, 53

CLIDELL, DADDY, and his role in the autobiography, 18–19, 23

COMMUNITY, as theme, 10, 19–20, 22, 27, 28–31, 36, 39–40, 49–50, 53–54

CULLINAN, MRS., and her role in the autobiography, 15, 52–53

DISPLACEMENT, as theme, 10, 26, 33, 45–48

FLOWERS, MRS. BERTHA, influence of, on Angelou, 14–15, 22, 30–31, 40, 52, 55

FREEMAN, MR.: Angelou molested by, 13; Angelou raped by, 7, 13–14, 16, 22, 35–36, 39–43, 50–53, 55–56, 59

GATHERING TOGETHER IN MY NAME: composition of, 45; denouement of, 36; and how it compares, 27, 30, 49

HEART OF A WOMAN, THE, and how it compares, 33, 49

I KNOW WHY THE CAGED BIRD SINGS: black culture celebrated in, 39–40, 44–45; blues tradition in, 28–30; denial of closure in, 43–45; epiphanic moment in, 31–33; fantasy in, 46–47;

gnosis in, 5–6; influence of church sermons on, 5; moral opposition to, 56–59; as novel-like, 24–25, 35–36; opening of, 10, 25–26, 31–32, 37, 51; oppositions within, 59; pathos of, 5, 29–30; racial self-hatred in, 31–32; and slave narratives, 5; as spiritual autobiography, 5–6; unique qualities of, 28–31; use of memory in, 10

JOHNSON, BAILEY, JR.: adolescence of, 20; Angelou's love for, 22, 36, 39; disappearance of, 15; first love of, 17; and his role in the autobiography, 10–22

HENDERSON, WILLIE, and his role in the autobiography, 10, 15, 16, 22, 39

LINCOLN, DR., as emblem of racism, 18, 46–47

LOUIS, JOE, and his role as cultural figure, 16, 40

MAKE, VUSUMZI, Angelou's marriage to, 7, 34

MOMMA (MRS. ANNIE HENDERSON): Angelou's relationship with, 45–48; limitations of, 30, 46; religious faith of, 10, 17, 22, 28–31; self-respect of, 11–12, 22, 40; as source of strength, 11–12, 22, 39, 44–48

MOTHER DEAR (VIVIAN BAXTER): Angelou's meeting with, 12; and blues tradition, 28–30; Momma compared to, 38; physical beauty of, 12, 15, 18, 22–23, 39; and white beauty standards, 15, 50; as word-bringer, 37–38

MOTHERHOOD, as theme, 34, 37–38, 43–48

ST. LOUIS, MISSOURI: Angelou's arrival in, 12; Stamps compared to, 39, 47–48

SEXISM, as theme, 20, 26, 34, 26

SINGIN' AND SWINGIN' AND GETTIN' MERRY LIKE CHRISTMAS, and how it compares, 45, 49

SOUTHERN CALIFORNIA, Angelou's experience in, 18, 48

STAMPS, ARKANSAS: Angelou's arrival in, 10; Angelou's return to, 14, 40; barrenness of, 14; community ritual in, 29–31, 40, 44–45, 49, 53–54; Depression in, 12; individualism in, 30–31; pathos of, 29–30; poverty in, 16, 29, 49; "powhitetrash" in, 11–12; revival meeting in, 15–16; St. Louis compared to, 39, 47–48; "whitefolks" in, 11, 16